NAVIGATING THE GREAT RECESSION

IMMIGRANT FAMILIES' STORIES OF RESILIENCE

ANA SÁNCHEZ-MUÑOZ
TRACY L. BUENAVISTA
EUNAI SHRAKE
GINA MASEQUESMAY

Kendall Hunt
publishing company

Cover art by Raymundo M. Hernandez

Kendall Hunt
publishing company

www.kendallhunt.com
Send all inquiries to:
4050 Westmark Drive
Dubuque, IA 52004-1840

ISBN 978-0-7575-9538-7

Printed in the United States of America
10 9 8 7 6 5 4 3 2

CONTENTS

FOREWORD

Juana Mora

The global economic recession that began in 2007 and is currently in a slow recovery has affected many U.S. families and individuals. Yet, there are some, as this book indicates, who have suffered extreme effects of the recession, including immigrants, working class individuals, and immigrant students. If the recession has taught us anything, it should be that we are all connected. That what happens here affects others. That other countries depend on our tourism dollars, we depend on the work of immigrants, and immigrant families depend on the remittances sent home from the United States. The economic downturn in the United States, for example, had an immediate effect on Mexico's economy, which experienced a reduction in tourism and remittances sent to families. By late 2008 and early 2009, the Mexican GDP had fallen by over 8% and unemployment increased by 6%.[1,2]

The impact of this economic downturn in the home country was that immigrants living in the United States could not even consider returning to their home country because the economic situation there was just as bad as it is here. Many decided to stay and ride out the crisis. So, how do immigrants, especially those who come from Latin America and Asian countries, cope with the economic ups and downs of a host country? In many ways, as this book illustrates, they cope by relying on each other, on strong community social networks here and in their home countries, and on their beliefs and hopes for a better future for themselves and their children.

In the United States, Latino and Asian immigrant families, children, and students have been hit hard by the recession, experiencing higher levels of unemployment; loss of jobs; increased student tuition; increased rent, food, and gas prices; and loss of homes. Before the recession, Asian and Latino immigrants

---

[1] Leah Muse-Orlinoff and Lewin Fischer, "Introduction," in *Mexican Migration and the U.S. Economic Crisis: A Transnational Perspective* (San Diego: University of California, 2010).

[2] Jacob Blanc, et al., "Making Do with Less: Current Economic Strategies in a Traditional Migrant-Sending Community," in *Recession without Borders: Mexican Migrants Confront the Economic Downturn* (San Diego: University of California, 2011).

struggled to learn a new language and culture, both necessary for a positive adaptation in a new economic and cultural environment. When the recession hit, these individuals were the "first fired"—the first to suffer loss of jobs, reductions in work hours, and loss of homes through foreclosures. However, as the stories of survival and adaptation in this book illustrate, the collectivist traditions and willingness to work hard have resulted in some amazing methods of survival and resilience. In addition, the economic recession has brought some individuals, families, and groups, such as students, together to create spaces to educate and advocate for themselves and others. Institutional responses, at times, have also served to help some individuals survive the crisis. As we read in these stories and as research indicates, institutional support is important for the ability of immigrants to survive economic stresses. However, the kind of institutional support needed and asked for is not a reliance on U.S. social welfare programs but rather support to become educated and to learn English in order to become self-sufficient. As reported by Cabrera-Hernandez et al.[3] in a study of Mexican immigrants from Tlacuitapenses, Jalisco, only 5% use food stamps, 6% receive unemployment benefits, and none in this study reported receiving welfare assistance. Instead, immigrants tend to reproduce the strong social networks that they bring from their home country and use these to adapt, find new jobs, open small businesses, and give each other loans in order to survive and thrive despite the recession.

The authors of this book have gathered stories about the impact of the economic recession on Latino and Asian immigrant families, couples, children, and students. The impact of the recession on people comes alive through these stories, and we can feel the pain of loss and the pride in survival. These essays tell us how a sister supports another sister with rent, household expenses, and childcare so that one of them can stay in school. They tell us about a young Asian woman who, by serving as a language broker for her family, suffers the knowledge of her families' financial troubles that cause her parents to divorce. Yet, by serving as the family language broker (translating unemployment documents for her family), she learns to advocate for her family and herself and find new supportive relationships through her Korean church. We learn of immigrant parents who work more than one job, who make do with less, go out less, and do what they have to do—in some cases, letting go of their home to foreclosure—in order to feed and educate their children. We learn about the effects of the economic stress on parents who calm this stress through alcohol and tobacco use and the effects of this on the further loss of one parent through illness. We also learn of the

---

[3] Jose Cabrera-Hernandez et al., "Coping with Hard Times in *El Norte,*" in *Recession Without Borders: Mexican Migrants Confront the Economic Downturn* (San Diego: University of California, 2011).

struggles of immigrant university students who cannot rely on family for financial support, but instead have to work to assist the family. Yet, through these struggles, minor miracles seem to happen, such as when a peer mentoring job on the campus helps one immigrant student stay in school and support her family. Another struggling student finds out that counseling is available free of charge on the campus and takes advantage of this and heals himself in order to help his family. I hope that this book creates a sense of our global connectedness so that we can support immigrant communities in our neighborhoods, schools, and places of employment and understand that we benefit from their presence as much and perhaps even more than they benefit from being here.

Bibliography

Blanc, Jacob, Israel Montiel Armas, Maria De La Paz Iglesias, Daniela Arizaga, and Luz Angelica Catano Corona. "Making Do with Less: Current Economic Strategies in a Traditional Migrant-Sending Community." In *Recession Without Borders: Mexican Migrants Confront the Economic Downturn.* Edited by David Scott FitzGerald, Rafael Alarcón, and Leah Muse-Orlinoff. San Diego: University of California, 2011.

Cabrera-Hernandez, Jose, Andrew Hall, Jessica De Anda, David Rocha Romero, and Raul Saldana. "Coping with Hard Times in *El Norte.*" In *Recession Without Borders: Mexican Migrants Confront the Economic Downturn.* Edited by David Scott FitzGerald, Rafael Alarcón, and Leah Muse-Orlinoff. San Diego: University of California, 2011.

Muse-Orlinoff, Leah, and Pedro Lewin-Fischer. "Introduction." In *Mexican Migration and the U.S. Economic Crisis: A Transnational Perspective.* Edited by Wayne Cornelius, David FitzGerald, Pedro Lewin Fischer, and Leah Muse-Orlinoff. San Diego: University of California, 2010.

ACKNOWLEDGMENTS

In 2008, we published a collection[1] of our students' stories of struggle journeying to America and adapting to a new culture and language because we felt it was important to share these stories with other students and teachers. Now, in light of the deep economic recession and its devastating effects on many of our students, we get together to give voice once again to those that are often silenced: working-class, immigrant, and racial/ethnic minority communities. As the project evolved, we now have Dr. Tracy Lachica Buenavista as co-editor along with Dr. Ana Sánchez-Muñoz, Dr. Eunai Shrake, and Dr. Gina Masequesmay. Dr. Juana Mora, who was the main editor of our 2008 book, was unable to participate in this collection due to other commitments. However, we are very grateful to her for writing the foreword to the present volume. We want to thank all the contributors for sharing their stories. We want to also thank Joseph Wells, our acquisition editor, and Wendy Pauly, our project coordinator, for their support and encouragement. We also want to thank and acknowledge the artwork of Raymundo Hernández, who designed our book cover. He is one of the many resilient immigrants who continue to fight for a more just world and are the focus of this book.

[1] Juana Mora, Gina Masequesmay, Eunai Shrake, and Ana Sánchez-Muñoz, *Learning English/Learning America: Latino and Asian American Voices* (Dubuque, IA: Kendall/Hunt, 2008).

INTRODUCTION

Navigating the Great Recession: Immigrants and Resilience

Ana Sánchez-Muñoz

The Economic Crisis and the Immigrant Population

The recent economic meltdown known as ***The Great Recession*** or simply ***The Recession*** is the biggest financial crisis in the United States since the Great Depression of the 1930s. In the words of Chairman of the Federal Reserve, Ben Bernanke, it is "the worst financial crisis in modern history." According to The National Bureau of Economic Research (NBER), the recession officially began in December 2007 and technically ended in June 2009.[1] However, the effects of The Great Recession continue to hurt the average American.

Unemployment remains high, fluctuating between 9.4% and 10.1%, between 2009 to the present,[2] with consumer demand, the housing sector, and bank lending all remaining weak. While most Americans are impacted by the economic crisis, the reports of the NBER and other official agencies fail to recognize how the recession has exacerbated the social, political, and economic disparities already hurting America's most vulnerable populations—the working class, minority, and immigrant communities. While these groups have always been more subject to situational risk factors, such as poverty or homelessness, the severity of the current economic conditions significantly increases for immigrant communities at a disproportionate rate. For example, in 2009, when the unemployment rate was

[1] "Business Cycle Dating Committee," *NBER,* last modified September 20, 2010, http://www.nber.org/cycles/sept2010.html.

[2] Bureau of Labor Statistics, accessed February 20, 2011, http://www.bls.gov/home.htm.

at its highest point in twenty years, Latinos were losing their jobs faster than any other group.[3]

The U.S. immigrant population (foreign-born) has increased from 9.6 million, or 4.7% of the population, in 1970, to 31.1 million or 11.1% in 2000.[4] Currently, the immigrant population represents 12.5% of the total population.[5] However, unaccounted for is the substantial number of undocumented persons residing in the United States. In fact, approximately 30% of the foreign-born population are "unauthorized" immigrants. Given the significant number of immigrant families (both naturalized and non-naturalized), it is important that we look at the impact of the financial crisis on immigrants. While many immigrants experience socioeconomic disparities, poverty rates are much higher among undocumented immigrants: the poverty rate for undocumented immigrant adults is 21%, or one in five; in contrast, the poverty rate is 13% for other immigrant adults, and 10% for U.S.-born adults.[6]

Many immigrant families live in communities struck by hardship with less resources and little access to a variety of basic rights like quality education and healthcare. There are also challenges associated with racial, linguistic, and social discrimination that minorities confront on a daily basis. In conversations with immigrant participants for our research, we heard many stories of what it is like to grow up coping with various forms of social inequity and with the feeling that the "American Dream" is not meant for everyone. Although most expressed that life is a journey that presents opportunities as well as challenges, minority immigrants like Claudio often highlighted the obstacles:

> *When I was five, all I wanted was to be friends with Chad Beatty. The closest I ever came was going over to his house after school and watching all of the other kids play with G. I. Joes and Hot Wheels; I was only allowed to sit on the porch in a white wicker chair. Chad's parents didn't want their son playing with a "dirty Mexican." Being five has its challenges, but being five when you are Mex-*

---

[3] Rakesh Kochhar, "Unemployment Rises Sharply Among Latino Immigrants in 2008," *Pew Hispanic Center,* 2009, http://pewhispanic.org/files/reports/102.pdf. Kochhar notes that the unemployment rate for Latino immigrants increased from 5.1% to 8.0%, or by 2.9 percentage points, from the fourth quarter of 2007 to the fourth quarter of 2008. During this same time period, the unemployment rate for all persons in the labor market increased from 4.6% to 6.6%, or by 2.0 percentage points.

[4] Thomas A. Gryn and Luke J. Larsen, "Nativity Status and Citizenship in the United States: 2009," *American Community Survey Briefs,* October 2010, http://www.census.gov/prod/2010pubs/acsbr09-16.pdf.

[5] *American Community Survey Data,* accessed March 22, 2011, http://www.census.gov/acs/www/.

[6] Jeffrey S. Passel and D'Vera Cohn, "A Portrait of Unauthorized Immigrants in the United States," *Pew Hispanic Center,* 2009, http://pewhispanic.org/reports/report.php?ReportID=107.

> *ican American, have no money, a gang member for a father, and a studio apartment that you share with your parents, grandparents, uncle, two aunts, and their boyfriends is just "a little bit" harder.*

Claudio's childhood memories offer a glimpse of multiple forms of oppression—racism and classism, among others—that many immigrant and minority groups face within the United States. For these communities, racism intersects with language, immigration status, ethnicity, culture, and identity issues that form layers of subordination to which members must either conform or resist. But with these stories of pain and struggle, we also discover examples of achievement that provide a message of hope. Our goal is to give voice to immigrant and working class communities with this book and to offer a space for immigrant families to share their stories of resilience and resistance in the shadow of The Great Recession.

Resilience and Immigrant Populations

The concept of ***resilience*** refers, in a general sense, to the capacity to cope with stress and difficulties. Individuals who are able not only to survive but also to prosper despite adverse circumstances are said to be ***resilient.*** Most research on resilience has concentrated on the individual protective factors of children and adolescents, such as good temperament or strong self-efficacy. In many of the studies on resilience (largely conducted in the fields of psychology and education), researchers focus on resilient individuals who have the ability to thrive despite being exposed to serious adverse life circumstances.[7] They analyze the personality traits that help particular individuals succeed when compared to a less resilient person. Claudio's narrative provides an excellent example of individual resilience that relies on conditioning among other factors to predict successful coping. For example, Claudio tells us how he was able to make it through adolescence with an alcoholic mother, a drug-addicted father, little or no support from other family members, and virtually no encouragement from school mates and friends. He learned to be a fighter and escape a gang life because he drew strength from his intense desire to have a better life than his parents. This focus on the individual has been identified in the literature as the first wave of research in resilience.[8]

---

[7] Sue Hartman and Adam Winsler, "Resiliency," in *Encyclopedia of Human Development* 3 (Thousand Oaks, CA: Sage, 2006).

[8] Margaret O'Doughterty Wright and Ann S. Masten, "Resilience Processes in Development: Fostering Positive Adaptation in the Context of Adversity," in *The Handbook of Resilience in Children,* ed. Sam Goldstein and Robert Brooks (New York: Kluwer Academic/Plenum Publishers, 2005).

As we sift through the literature on resilience, we see how it evolves from a psychological concept of individual developmental asset, the individual capacity to bounce back from adversities, to a more sociological and ecological formulation of adaptive processes that account for family and community resources. The second wave accounts for a more dynamic view on resilience, which looks at the context of adversity and the relations between individuals and the systems in which they function to positively adapt to the environment. In this evolution, a new emphasis on an intervention model in developmental pathways was advocated and soon followed by a more micro-level of analysis to explore the gene-environment for intervention. The third wave examines ways to foster resilience and opens the door to preventive and interventionist models.[9] An attempt to integrate the different levels of analyses was categorized as a fourth wave in the research on resilience.[10] It is at this point that the fourth wave incorporates different levels of analysis, which are focused on the integration of research and prevention efforts across disciplines. Applying the notion of resilience to immigrant research and critical Ethnic Studies, in this book we ask readers to consider an emergent fifth wave of research, which views resilience as a manifestation of community cultural wealth, resistance, and transformation.[11]

Toward a New Wave of Resilience Research: Resilience as Resistance

Despite the recognition of social contexts in understanding resilience, most work still views it as an individual adaptive process. However, resilience can be examined beyond individual coping and survival; it can also be investigated in the context of ***resistance*** that aims to produce larger changes within society. Education research grounded in Critical Race Theory (CRT) argues that the normative discourse on resilience has pathologized youth of color who do not conform to white middle-class notions of adaptive behaviors.[12,13,14] Emphasizing the significance of social identities and collective experiences, works from critical youth

---

[9] Ann S. Masten, "Resilience in developing systems: Progress and promise as the fourth wave rises," *Development and Psychopathology* 19 no. 3 (2007): 921–930.

[10] Ibid.

[11] Tara J. Yosso, *Critical Race Counterstories along the Chicana/Chicano Educational Pipeline* (New York: Routledge, 2006).

[12] Michael Ungar, "Families as Navigators and Negotiators: Facilitating Culturally and Contextually Specific Expressions of Resilience," *Family Process* 49, no. 3 (2010): 421–435.

[13] Dorothy Bottrell, "Understanding 'Marginal' Perspectives: Toward Social Theory of Resilience," *Qualitative Social Work* 8 (2009): 321.

[14] Daniel Solórzano and Dolores Delgado Bernal, "Examining Transformational Resistance through a Critical race and LatCrit Theory Framework. Chicana and Chicano Student in an Urban Context," *Urban Education* 36, no. 2 (2001): 308–342.

Photograph 1 CSUN student protests, March 2, 2011.

studies and CRT have reconceptualized resilience as resistance. By giving voice to marginalized youth and viewing them as having agency, we can analyze how they confront inequality and how their resilience is built through practices of resistance to protect against stereotyping and stigma. This is the perspective from which resilience is analyzed in our book, which following recent research in critical studies, challenges the assumptions of standardized outcomes associated with normative resilience and development.[15]

In this volume, we provide examples of immigrants navigating the financial crisis by engaging in various forms of resistance through community organization, education, and peaceful demonstrations. One powerful example is the series of student protests that took place throughout California on March 4, 2010, and March 2 and April 13, 2011 (see Photograph 1). To demonstrate against spiraling fee hikes in public higher education[16] that threaten to make it unaffordable for

[15] Bottrell, "Understanding 'Marginal' Perspectives," 231.

[16] In the State of California, the public education system has suffered severe cuts because of the state's financial problems. Layoffs and furloughs have hit many districts and school systems, along with reductions in course offerings and grants.

many students, thousands took to the streets throughout California to voice their concerns and to communicate to those in government that education is a right and not a privilege of the upper class. As civil rights activist, Reverend James Lawson said on March 2, 2011, to a crowd of CSUN protesters, "It is the role of the government, society, and institutions to serve the next generation and allow them to achieve their fullest potential."[17]

Fee hikes affect undocumented students of color even more deeply since their legal status remains uncertain (see Section 2 of this book). As AB540 student and community organizer Raymundo Hernández states in his story:

> *Fees continue to rise, it is becoming increasingly difficult for undocumented students to attend and remain in school. Although I, as well as other undocumented students face many uncertainties, we hope that educational access can help us to survive this harsh economic situation.*

Lawson and Hernández' statements underscore the idea that communities of color possess an important social critique regarding the ways in which the economic crisis has exacerbated their social, economic, and political conditions. It is this critique that is the tie that binds the narratives we highlight in this collection.

Stories of Resilient Immigrants during The Great Recession: Resistance and Social Change

In this book, we concentrate on three areas of support for our analysis of resilience as resistance: familial, institutional, and social and community networks. Many immigrants are able to endure severe economic adversity because they can draw on a complex network of support, which includes financial and emotional help from family (stories in Section 1) and ethnic community members (stories in Section 3). Additionally, the stories collected in this book remind us that the aid provided by state and local institutions is fundamental to the survival of immigrant populations (stories in Section 2). Unfortunately, in a time of global economic meltdowns, these necessary resources are at risk of being severely cut or disappearing altogether, and it is this context that serves as the backdrop to the stories of resilience presented in this book.

Members of different immigrant communities wrote all the stories in this collection. Most of the stories are written from the perspective of immigrants themselves or members (children and partners) of immigrant families and

[17] Reverend James Lawson in an address to CSUN protesters, March 2, 2011.

communities. These perspectives are important in that they are rarely considered in discourse on immigrants. In this sense, the narratives represent what education scholars Daniel Solórzano and Tara Yosso define as "counter-story,"[18] a method of bringing to light the stories of people whose voices are often marginalized.[19] We argue that among the hardest hit by The Great Recession are members from immigrant communities. Yet, among research that attempts to uncover how people in the United States are affected by the economic crisis, stories from immigrant communities either remain absent or do not focus on their resilience. Three of the editors in this collection are immigrants, and one is second-generation. This book represents our attempt to mediate this gap in the literature.

We present personal stories of a diverse group of immigrants who are able to survive the crisis thanks not only to their individual resilience but also to the assistance of a number of resources, including public assistance and community support. Some of the questions guiding the stories include: Given the current recession in the United States, how are immigrant communities and individuals overcoming the increased disadvantageous conditions they find themselves in? What are some of the coping techniques that will allow them to be resilient and, in turn, be able to constructively respond to future adversity? In which ways are resilient immigrants resisting patterns of oppression and becoming agents of social change? In thinking about the ways in which the stories address these questions, we hope to encourage readers to better understand the relationship between The Great Recession, resilience, and, more broadly, resistance among immigrant communities.

Bibliography

Bottrell, Dorothy. "Understanding 'Marginal' Perspectives: Toward Social Theory of Resilience." *Qualitative Social Work* 8, no. 3 (September 2009): 321–339.

Gryn, Thomas A., and Luke J. Larsen. "Nativity Status and Citizenship in the United States: 2009." *American Community Survey Briefs*. October 2010. http://www.census.gov/prod/2010pubs/acsbr09-16.pdf.

Hartman, Sue, and Adam Winsler. "Resiliency." In *Encyclopedia of Human Development* 3, 1075–1077. Ed. Neil J. Salkind. Thousand Oaks, CA: Sage, 2006.

---

[18] Daniel Solórzano and Tara Yosso, "Critical Race Methodology: Counterstorytelling as an Analytical Framework for Education Research," *Qualitative Inquiry* 8 (2002):36.

[19] Ibid., 32.

Kochhar, Rakesh. "Unemployment Rises Sharply Among Latino Immigrants in 2008." *Pew Hispanic Center.* 2009. http://pewhispanic.org/files/reports/102.pdf.

Masten, Ann S. "Resilience in developing systems: Progress and promise as the fourth wave rises." *Development and Psychopathology* 19, no. 3 (2007): 921–930.

O'Doughterty Wright, Margaret, and Ann S. Masten. "Resilience Processes in Development: Fostering Positive Adaptation in the Context of Adversity." In *The Handbook of Resilience in Children,* 17–37. Eds. Sam Goldstein and Robert Brooks. New York: Kluwer Academic/Plenum Publishers, 2005.

Solórzano, Daniel, and Dolores Delgado Bernal. "Examining Transformational Resistance through a Critical Race and LatCrit Theory Framework. Chicana and Chicano Student in an Urban Context." *Urban Education* 36, no. 2 (2001): 308–342.

Solórzano, Daniel, and Tara Yosso. "Critical Race Methodology: Counterstorytelling as an Analytical Framework for Education Research." *Qualitative Inquiry* 8 (2002): 23–44. DOI: 10.1177/107780040200800103.

Ungar, Michael. "Families as Navigators and Negotiators: Facilitating Culturally and Contextually Specific Expressions of Resilience." *Family Process* 49, no. 3 (2010): 421–435.

Yosso, Tara J. *Critical Race Counterstories along the Chicana/Chicano Educational Pipeline*. New York: Routledge, 2006.

SECTION 1

Resilience and Immigrant Families

Eunai Shrake

People tend to show remarkable resilience when faced with significant difficulties and hardships. As the saying goes, "When the going gets tough, the tough get going." Dealing with hardships or staying resilient is particularly apparent among immigrant populations who often experience challenges to thrive in new environments.[1] What enables them to effectively navigate an adverse environment? How do people's strategies to cope with adversity reflect cultural differences? These are particularly acute questions to ask in a time of economic recession when immigrant families and students experience hardships from many sides, related to their finances, employment, fee increases, and class enrollment. In this section, students from immigrant backgrounds share how they are under various pressures but still have the capacity to respond to adverse economic conditions in efforts to be resilient.

There are many factors that contribute to one's resilience. For example, individuals weather adversity more effectively and stay resilient when they have a wider repertoire of personal as well as environmental resources at hand, such as positive self-concept, persistence, moral and spiritual resources, the support of others, and supportive systems in their community.[2] However, many studies suggest that the primary factor in fostering one's resilience is supportive family relationships. Relationships in the family provide positive role models, offer emotional and

---

[1] Vivian Tseng, "Family Interdependence and Academic Adjustment in College: Youth from Immigrant and U.S.-Born Families," *Child Development* 75, no. 3 (2004): 966–983.

[2] Michael Rutter, "Psychosocial Resilience and Protective Mechanisms," *American Journal of Orthopsychiatry* 57 (1987): 316–331.

financial support, and help to maintain a positive outlook for the future despite adversity.[3]

A caring and supportive family relationship is a particularly important adjustment strategy for immigrants who seek to gain a firm foothold in the United States through the sharing and pooling of resources. In this section, we focus on the role of immigrant families in helping to shape immigrant resilience by looking at various ways that students from immigrant backgrounds utilize their families as a resilience strategy.

Immigrant Families: Cultural Deficit or Bulwark of Resistance?

Traditionally, immigrant families are often viewed as deficient—a characteristic that explains their subordination in American society.[4] Social science research rooted in this narrative looked at immigrant families as social problems by pointing out their presumed inability to assimilate with American society. Grown out of the dominant assimilationist school of race relations, this approach overemphasized different patterns and relationships in immigrant families that deviate from the norms and expectations of mainstream American culture in order to present differences in immigrant family systems as deviant and pathological. Moreover, the social science research entrenched in this cultural deficiency perspective focused attention on immigrant family malfunctioning such as "family role reversals"[5] and intergenerational conflict. In doing so, they portrayed Asian American and Latino families as sites of conflict and problem and less as a resource that individuals actively shape and mobilize for survival and resistance.[6]

In contrast to this cultural deficit perspective, more recent research indicates how immigrant families often operate to compensate for resources withheld by the larger society. This family systems approach considers the immigrant family as an open system through which immigrants cope with socioeconomic marginality[7]

---

[3] Froma Walsh, "A Family Resilience Framework: Innovative Practice Applications," *Family Relations* 51 (2002): 130–137.

[4] Maxine Zinn and Angela Y.H. Pok, "Tradition and Transition in Mexican-Origin Families," in *Minority Families in the United States: A Multicultural Perspective,* ed. Ronald L. Taylor (Upper Saddle River, NJ: Prentice Hall, 1998).

[5] Christine Yeh, Angela Kim, Stephanie Pituc, and Mark Atkins, "Poverty, Loss, and Resilience: The Story of Chinese Immigrant Youth," *Journal of Counseling Psychology* 25, no. 1 (2008): 34–48.

[6] Evelyn N. Glenn with Stacey G.H. Yap, "Chinese American Families," in *Minority Families in the United States: A Multicultural Perspective,* ed. Ronald L. Taylor (Upper Saddle River, NJ: Prentice Hall, 1998).

[7] Zinn and Pok, *op cit.,* p. 94.

and resist the demoralizing effects of poverty and discrimination. From this theoretical perspective, the immigrant family is viewed as a site of resistance and empowerment rather than a site of deprivation or domination. In other words, the immigrant family functions as a "counterspace"[8] that provides a place of comfort, nurturance, and building communities of resistance. As a counterspace[9], the immigrant family mediates stress and enables family members to surmount hardship and prevail over adversity. Looking at resilient family functioning through a systemic lens calls us to view individual resilience as embedded in family process and mutual influence.[10] It is through the coping and adaptation processes in the family that individual resilience is fostered.

It is clear that family is a very important factor in the development of resilience in individuals. Now, the question is how immigrant families help individuals develop resilience. In other words, what are the family mechanisms embedded in family relationships and processes that enable individuals to develop resilience? In the next section, we will focus on various ways that immigrant families help foster resilience in immigrant individuals.

The Role of Family in Shaping Resilience

One of the important roles of family in shaping immigrant resilience is to provide **emotional support** to its members. Emotional support means the availability of a person with whom one can discuss problems and share personal worries.[11] Members of the immediate family frequently provide emotional support through encouragement, reassurance, and high expectations. Through family members' encouragement and expectations, one learns to believe in oneself and in one's future, developing the critical resilience traits of self-worth, personal strength, and optimism. In this way, emotional support provided by family members reduces the impact of negative life events and bolsters one's resilience.[12]

---

[8] Daniel Solórzano and Dolores Degaldo Bernal, "Examining Transformational Resistance through a Critical Race and LatCrit Theory Framework: Chicana and Chicano Students in an Urban Context," *Urban Education* 36, no. 3 (2001): 308–342.

[9] The term *counterspace* refers to a literal and figurative place where people of color resist oppression and empower themselves to become change agents.

[10] Froma Walsh, *Strengthening Family Resilience* (New York, NY: Guilford Press, 2006).

[11] Thomas A. Willis, Elaine A. Blechman, and Grace McNamara, "Family Support, Coping, and Competence," in *Stress, Coping, and Resiliency in Children and Families,* eds. Mavis E. Hetherington and Elaine A. Blechman (Mahwah, NJ: Lawrence Erlbaum, 1996).

[12] Mavis E. Hetherington and Elaine A. Blechman, "Introduction and Overview," in *Stress, Coping, and Resiliency in Children and Families,* eds. Mavis E. Hetherington and Elaine A. Blechman (Mahwah, NJ: Lawrence Erlbaum, 1996).

Immigrant families also help shape individual resilience through **pooling or sharing resources.** Pooling resources entails a family-based exchange of labor, financial capital, housing, job referrals, and other information. Pooling or sharing resources within the family is a commonly reported coping strategy for economic hardship among immigrant populations. Nazli Kibria described this immigrant family economic strategy of bringing disparate resources into the family more adequately with the term *patchworking,* which presents "an image of jagged pieces of assorted material stitched together in a sometimes haphazard and uncalculated fashion."[13] Patchworking demonstrates immigrant families' resourcefulness, and many immigrants rely on this collective coping strategy to persevere through economic hardship.

Another way that immigrant families contribute to the shaping of individual resilience is to provide **intergenerational role models.** Historically, the family has been a conduit for cultural transmission, passing on cultural beliefs and traditions from one generation to another.[14] This includes the mediation of the older generation's past experiences of coping with adverse life situations. In other words, legacies of previous crises in the multigenerational family system influence how individuals respond to contemporary adverse situation.[15] As Froma Walsh states, "resilience is woven in a web of relationships and experiences over the course of the life cycle and across the generations."[16] The intergenerational process of transmission is particularly apparent in refugee populations where parents' past experiences of overcoming tremendous hardship provides a model and moral compass for shaping children's resilience. Through this intergenerational exchange, younger generations look up to their parents as role models to find heightened appreciation for life and draw inspiration, comfort, guidance, and a means of coping with and resisting disadvantageous economic and social conditions. This process of intergenerational role modeling is the way in which immigrant individuals maintain a hopeful outlook for the future despite adversity and oppression.

---

[13] Nazli Kibria, *Family Tightrope: The Changing Lives of Vietnamese Americans* (Princeton, NJ: Princeton University Press, 1993).

[14] Hamilton I. McCubbin, Marilyn A. McCubbin, Anne I. Thompson, and Elizabeth A. Thompson, "Resiliency in Ethnic Families: A Conceptual Model for Predicting Family Adjustment and Adaptation," in *Resiliency in Native American and Immigrant Families,* eds. Hamilton I. McCubbin, Elizabeth A. Thompson, Anne I. Thompson, and Julie E. Fromer (Thousand Oaks, CA: Sage Publications, 1998).

[15] Betty Carter and Monica McGoldrick (Eds.), *The Expanded Family Life Cycle: Individual, Family, and Social Perspectives* (Boston, MA: Allyn and Bacon, 1999).

[16] Froma Walsh, 2006, *op cit.,* p. 12.

In summary, immigrant families contribute to cultivating resilience in individual members of the family in various ways, which include providing emotional support, sharing resources, and providing intergenerational role models. Utilizing these various family functions to navigate financial hardship, the student narratives in this chapter depict how they have survived "The Great Recession" and resisted social disadvantages.

Immigrant Students' Stories of Resilience with Family Support

In the stories presented in this section, the authors describe the challenges they faced in this time of "The Great Recession," as well as how they utilized their families as a resilience strategy. The prevalent theme in the students' narratives was the impact of the current economic recession on their educational opportunities, quality of family life, job opportunities, and the ways their immigrant family helped boost their resilience. As such, these student narratives contain examples of how immigrant families function as a "counterspace"—a site of resilience building.

In the first story, Kevan Moscoso, a Korean-born adoptee with Filipino American and Japanese American parents, describes how the current economic meltdown seriously constrained his ability to graduate on time. In his story he explains how state educational budget cuts facilitated a reduction in course offerings and a schedule in which he worked full-time and attended school part-time. Despite all this, Kevan refuses to give up and claims that the main source of his spirit of resilience is emotional support from his parents who show faith and hope in him and provide assurance and encouragement for him to not give up under any circumstance.

Similarly, Yaneli Gonzalez, a 1.5-generation Chicana, begins her story with a depiction of her family's financial difficulty caused by a change in her mother's employment status. She goes on to discuss how fee hikes, limited courses, overcrowded classrooms, and her inability to receive financial aid made it difficult to continue her education. While her family cannot provide any financial support, like Kevan, they provide an emotional support that fuels her resilience. She writes, "I know that my family is always there for me. It is their unconditional love, support, faith, and prayers that have kept me alive in this game of survival of the fittest."

While the first two stories focus on the emotional support that helps to sustain their spirit of resilience, Gabriela Habi, a 1.5-generation Chicana, introduces the concept of "patchworking." She details how her family pooled resources together when they were hit by the economic recession. For example, when her father lost his job and had financial trouble, many family members chipped in to make mortgage payments and save their home from foreclosure. Such support was then extended to her sister who moved with her children to the family's home when she found herself in economic trouble. Through this sharing of residential place and pooling financial capital, Gabriela's story exemplifies how patchworking contributes to immigrant families' resilience in the economic tough times.

The next three stories depict intergenerational resilience. Yvonne Kwan, a second-generation Chinese American, presents a striking account of her father-in-law's escape from a Khmer Rouge death camp and how it provided a strong model of resilience for her and her husband. Yvonne begins her story with a depiction of her father-in-law's hardships as an escapee from the Khmer Rouge and a refugee in the United States. Then, like other students, she discusses fee hikes and the reduction of college course offerings in the current economic recession, which forced her husband to take a longer time to graduate. She finally relates the current hardship that she and her husband experience to her parents' struggles as immigrants and refugees in this country. In doing so, she explains how her father-in-law's legacy of resilience provided her and her husband with inspiration and courage to cope and stay resilient during the recession.

Similarly, Daisy Le, a second-generation Vietnamese American, also explores how her father's experience as a refugee provided her with not only inspiration but also a moral compass to persevere and achieve. For Daisy, her parents' past struggles motivate her to strive for success. With her parents as her confidants and positive role models, she maintains a hopeful outlook for the future despite the adversity.

In the last story of this chapter, Jane Shin, a 1.5-generation Korean American, presents her hard-working and sacrificing parents as positive role models who inspire her to learn to be resilient. Jane explains how her parents immigrated to provide her with a better educational opportunity. She then details her parents' struggles with language barriers and subsequent economic hardship in the United States, as well as her amazement in seeing her parents endure difficult times. Seeing her parents' continuous struggles and actions of resilience, she appears to acquire the strength and inspiration to overcome any obstacles in her life. In doing so, she shows the significance of intergenerational experiences in contributing to the resilience in immigrant individuals.

Conclusion

Students from immigrant backgrounds face significant challenges in the current "Great Recession"—job loss, higher tuition, fewer classes, and family finances.

They have been able to cope through persistence, moral and spiritual resources, and the support of others and their community. However, it is the strength within their familial structure that fosters for them the most resilience. Families offer positive role models, emotional and financial support, share and pool resources, and help them to maintain a positive outlook. Despite the negative stereotypes about immigrant families, they are instead caring and supportive, helping individuals shape and mobilize strategies for survival and resistance in the "counterspace" of the home.

Bibliography

Carter, Betty, and Monica McGoldrick (Eds.). *The Expanded Family Life Cycle: Individual, Family, and Social Perspectives.* Boston, MA: Allyn and Bacon, 1999.

Glenn, Evelyn Nakano, and Stacey G.H. Yap. "Chinese American Families." In *Minority Families in the United States: A Multicultural Perspective.* Ed. Ronald L. Taylor. Upper Saddle River, NJ: Prentice Hall, 1998.

Hetherington, E. Mavis, and Elaine A. Blechman (Eds.). *Stress, Coping, and Resiliency in Children and Families.* Mahwah, NJ: Lawrence Erlbaum, 1996.

Kibria, Nazli. *Family Tightrope: The Changing Lives of Vietnamese Americans.* Princeton, NJ: Princeton University Press, 1993.

McCubbin, Hamilton I., Marilyn A. McCubbin, Anne I. Thompson, and Elizabeth A. Thompson. "Resiliency in Ethnic Families: A Conceptual Model for Predicting Family Adjustment and Adaptation." In *Resiliency in Native American and Immigrant Families.* Eds, McCubbin, Hamilton I., Elizabeth A. Thompson, Anne I. Thompson, and Julie E. Fromer. Thousand Oaks, CA: Sage Publications, 1998.

Rutter, Michael. "Psychosocial Resilience and Protective Mechanisms." *American Journal of Orthopsychiatry* 57 (1987): 316–331.

Solórzano, Daniel, and Dolores Degaldo Bernal. "Examining Transformational Resistance through a Critical Race and LatCrit Theory Framework: Chicana and Chicano Students in an Urban Context." *Urban Education* 36, no. 3 (2001): 308–342.

Tseng, Vivian. "Family Interdependence and Academic Adjustment in College: Youth from Immigrant and U.S.-Born Families." *Child Development* 75, no. 3 (2004): 966–983.

Walsh, Froma. *Strengthening Family Resilience,* New York, NY: Guilford Press, 2006.

———. "A Family Resilience Framework: Innovative Practice Applications." *Family Relations* 51 (2002): 130–137.

Willis, Thomas A., Elaine A. Blechman, and Grace McNamara. "Family Support, Coping, and Competence." In *Stress, Coping, and Resiliency in Children and Families*. Eds. Hetherington E. Mavis and Elaine A. Blechman. Mahwah, NJ: Lawrence Erlbaum Associates, 1996.

Yeh, Christine, Angela Kim, Stephanie Pituc, and Mark Atkins, "Poverty, Loss, and Resilience: The Story of Chinese Immigrant Youth." *Journal of Counseling Psychology* 25, no. 1 (2008): 34–48.

Zinn, Maxine, and Angela Y.H. Pok. "Tradition and Transition in Mexican-Origin Families." In *Minority Families in the United States: A Multicultural Perspective*. Ed. Ronald L. Taylor. Upper Saddle River, NJ: Prentice Hall, 1998.

1

My Family in the Economic Tsunami

Kevan Moscoso

A flight for Korean Airlines landed on a bright summer day in July of 1986. Unaware of what was happening, Kevan took his first breath of American air and smiled warmly under the equally warming sunshine. This is the moment that I would like to go back to.

Kim Han Min was born on March 24, 1986, in Seoul, South Korea. Kim Han Min's biological parents were social outcasts in South Korea, because of their premarital relations that resulted in Han Min's birth. In South Korea, it was illegal for two people with the same surname to marry and start a family, no matter what their age and feelings were. Because they had the same surname, they couldn't get married. So, I was put up for adoption. I left Korea in July of 1986 and I left behind the name, "Kim Han Min" and all things Korean. My adoptive parents, or "real" parents as I like to call them, renamed me Kevan Jon Moscoso. In short, I am a 1.5 generation immigrant from South Korea, adopted into a family of a second-generation Filipino American man and third-generation Japanese American woman.

I was a small miracle to my family, and my parents expected me to be smart, industrious, and successful. These were the wishes of my parents and they have been instilled in me through positive reinforcement. My mother and father were willing to ensure my success no matter what the cost. My mom quit her job in order to stay home with me, and my dad took on extra hours to help us get by. Unfortunately, these wishes were snuffed at the beginning of the economic downturn.

My parents were born into middle-class families. My parents didn't grow up poor, but they were hardly able to afford more than what was necessary to everyday life and survival. My mom, Karen, is a third-generation Japanese American. My grandparents on my mother's side had a farm in northern California that was unfortunately forfeited during World War II. My great grandparents were interned along with my grandmother while my Nisei grandfather fought for the United States of America. Even after the war, my grandparents were never able to recover from the sudden loss of their property and their life practically. My mother went on to go to Los Angeles Valley College, while my grandparents worked hard and long hours to try to support the family. My dad, Ernest Moscoso, is a second-generation Filipino American. His father, Anselmo, passed away at a young age, and his mother, Fe, had to take the role of the head of household. She worked hard doing odd jobs around the neighborhood and struggled financially to keep her house.

This pattern of economic hardship didn't end with my grandparents' generation. My parents also fell victim to circumstance. My father, after serving in the United States Army, did not have any education beyond high school and had a hard time finding a job. He is currently a salesman for a small roofing company. My mother quit her job to take care of me when I was adopted. After I was old enough to be somewhat independent, my mother took a job in the school cafeteria at a local middle school. She was laid off in early 2000, because of cuts in the state's budget for education. Ever since this happened, my family has been on a wild rollercoaster, trying to be extra careful with money while not denying me the educational opportunities they felt would ensure a successful future for me.

It was two years ago when I realized that tuition was going up at an alarming rate. When I saw my tuition jump a few hundred dollars, I got alarmed and began to question the economy as a whole. I began to see the economy turn downward and the telltale signs of a recession on the horizon. As the economy began to turn downwards, people became less willing to spend, and this caused my father's salary to take a huge hit. My parents had to file for bankruptcy because my father's salary was dependent on sales. Just as my family was experiencing a serious economic hardship due to my father's diminished salary, everything around me seemed to become more expensive.

However, what affected me the most was the tuition hike. Because we were a family of three, barely scraping by, I was ineligible for federal student aid. I couldn't get a student loan because of my parents' recent bankruptcy and my insufficient credit. I felt I was stuck. I had to take a full-time job to pay my tuition and to help out my family as well. At first, I thought to myself, if I can make "x" amount of money in "x" amount of time, I'll be able to help my family keep the house, cars, and the debt collectors at bay. Unfortunately, I soon realized that 24 hours in one day wasn't enough to go to school full time and hold down a forty-plus hour a week job. I simply couldn't keep up with school while working full time. I ended up failing all of my classes that semester because I couldn't make it to class and complete all of the assignments. I came to a conclusion that my next semester would be different. So, I decided to go to school part time and keep my full-time job. This decision soon met its first road block, when I was let go from my job due to the failing economy and the failing banks. (I had been working for Washington Mutual at the time.) Having barely any money left after bills, I struggled to pay my way into school. I was able to save money by cutting out anything that wasn't a necessity, but this put a serious damper on my life.

The semester that followed was horrible as I saw my tuition rise exponentially again. This time, I thought I prepared and saved enough to afford full-time school. After reading about the new fees and the rising tuition, I realized I would only be able to take a part-time school load. This was very upsetting to my family. We could barely afford my schooling before, but now it was like the school was trying to trap me for as long as it could. I finally made peace with the idea that it would take me seven or more years to graduate, but the poor economy didn't only affect my bank account. It also affected my school as a whole. When I tried to enroll, I couldn't get into any classes in my underfunded major. Due to the budget cuts, my major department scaled back course offerings and lowered enrollment caps for most classes, making it difficult to enroll. Worse still, departmental capstone classes had been canceled due to the low enrollment. This just added more and more roadblocks to my goal of achieving a college degree. I am now in my sixth year of college, and things aren't looking better. I see my classes getting more and more crowded and the class offerings becoming less and less.

This didn't mean that all was lost. This didn't mean that I would simply roll over and play possum. My family wouldn't accept this, and I wouldn't accept this. I am a firm believer that anything is attainable through hard work and perseverance, but no burden should be shouldered alone. Through these tough times, I've found shelter in my parents' arms. Much like a child with a cut on his knee can be calmed and reassured that everything will be "okay" with a little kiss from mom, I too can say that my parents have been my rock in this unnerving tsunami. My parents are my inspiration and reason for persevering. They have shown me throughout my life that sacrifice and determination are necessary tools to survive. When times get the toughest, that's when one must ask for help. I am more than grateful to know that during these tough times, I am able to speak with my family and, in lieu of financial support, I have something far more valuable. I have a family that tells me anything is still possible if I work hard. It is this strong family support that has kept me positive in these tough times. I cannot express how valuable it is to have this kind of support. It is far beyond any material value. With this continued support from my family, I am sure I will persevere and finish college no matter what it takes.

2

Mi Familia in Times of Crisis

Yaneli Gonzalez

I was born in Tuxpan, Nayarit, Mexico. Tuxpan is a small town where I was raised by my grandmother, grandfather, and mother. I said I was raised by my grandparents too because my mother started making frequent trips to the United States since I was two years old leaving me behind with my grandparents. My mother made at least three trips to Los Angeles before she decided that this was where she wanted my brother and me to live. I was nine years old when I came to this country. My brother and I crossed the U.S.-Mexico border by ourselves with the help of a coyote. We left my grandmother and grandfather in Tijuana early in the morning and the coyote, who was a nice lady, took my brother and me in her car and headed to the border. I remember being nervous about crossing the border. Though I was too young to understand legal complications, I knew there was something wrong with being smuggled across the border, but somehow I managed to calm my nerves and made it through the border without being asked any questions. I longed to be with my mother so badly that every minute seemed like a thousand. I was terrified with the thought that I might never be able to see my mother again. I left my grandmother at about seven in the morning and it was not until four in the afternoon that my brother and I reunited with my mother. This day in September was the longest day of my life and one of the days that would change the course of my life forever.

I came to this country when I was nine years old, and I came as a Mexican citizen. I am now twenty-three years old and even though I am still a Mexican citizen, I have adopted and incorporated American culture into my identity. It is hard to say I am only Mexican because I am not. After living in another country and adopting the language and culture of this new country, it is hard to define myself as Mexican only. I define myself and my ethnicity as Chicana/Mexican-American/Mexicana. As probably reflected in the previous sentence, it was a struggle to define my identity. However, I have to say that though it was hard I figured it out and made peace with the two cultures and languages. I am a nice mixture of Mexican (Spanish and Aztec or other native South American cultures) with the redefined Mexican identity and culture in the U.S. Southwest, as well as Chicana and, of course, American. I struggled to balance all of the demands of these cultures, but I finally found the middle ground if there is such a place.

Growing up, not only did I struggle with my identity in terms of my ethnicity and culture, my family and I have also struggled financially. Ever since I came to this country my family was living with one income only. My stepfather was the only one that could work and provide for the family. Initially he did not allow my mother to work because he wanted her to spend time with my brother and me. After a couple of years the need for my mother to work became greater, but my mother, without any legal proof of her status in the United States, could not work. It was not until I finished high school that my mother, brother, and I became legal residents of this country, and then we could contribute to the household. My mother finally found a job about three years ago, and it looked very promising. But with the recession the company had to cut back on salaries so she went from being a good-salaried, full-time worker to a minimum-waged, hourly worker. The recession hit my family hard just when we thought we could all work together to achieve the "American Dream." With the recession, we had to tighten our belts and struggle to make ends meet once again. To make matters worse, my brother graduated from high school in the middle of the recession and was trying to apply to a private college. Although he gets some financial aid from school, it has been hard on the family since he lives in Oakland and only works a couple of hours a week. Obviously he had to take on student loans, but that is not enough, so my mother does what she can to help him. But with mother's low income, there is not much she could do for him.

The recession has also affected me on a personal level. I work part time and attend college full time. For some reason, I have not been able to get any financial aid for college. At first, it was because I was undocumented, but after I got my papers, I have no idea why I am not qualified for financial aid. I work at a bank so when the recession hit and there was talk about government's takeover of the banks or buyouts, my anxieties went through the roof. I was constantly worried that I could lose my job anytime, either tomorrow or next week. What would I do then? How could I pay for school? My mother would not be able to help me. I have been paying for my tuition and, without a job, how can I afford college tuition? I lived with this anxiety for about six months. I lived with the constant worry that I would lose my job and would not be able to afford college. Fortunately for me, I was able to keep my job, and the bank that I work for was not one of the banks that was bought out or taken over. But, of course, we all know it was one of the banks that received help from the federal government. Just when it seemed like I was out of the woods and I had saved just enough money to pay for my fall tuition, I received the bad news about fee hikes. At first, it was just rumors that tuition was going to be increased. I kept hoping that it would not be true, but one summer night as I was ready to go to bed, I checked my CSUN e-mail and there it was—an e-mail that said that tuition would be higher than the previous year. Once again my anxiety levels went to the roof. How was I going to make ends meet and make the extra $500 or so to pay for tuition? I had to borrow some money from my aunt to pay for my tuition in full. I was very upset, not only because I had to pay more for tuition, but also because the number of classes offered was being reduced and professors were forced to take furlough days. I was paying more to receive less instruction. On top of everything, I was not able to enroll in the classes that I needed to graduate. I tried to enroll in everything possible but, with limited classes, spaces, and professors not adding, I ended up taking whatever I could. I have to say I am lucky to have an advisor who was willing to work with me and substitute some classes in order for me to graduate on time.

I had to struggle throughout my life with family problems, self-esteem issues, and financial issues. At the age of twenty-three, I know that no matter what I do or where I go, I will always have that support group that has been with me since birth: my family. *Familia* (family) takes on a different meaning in times of hardship. *Familia* is not only blood-related relatives but also those people that you choose to be your family, such as friends. It is this *familia* that has helped me and continues to help me in times of crisis. When I feel hopeless, alone, depressed, or happy, I know that my family is always there for me. It is their unconditional love, support, faith, and prayers that have kept me alive in this game of survival of the fittest.

3

On Each Other's Shoulders

Gabriela Habi

I was born in a small town called Penjamo, in the state of Guanajuato in Mexico, to a family of five children. My twin sister and I would make it a family of seven children. I lived in a small house where my mother was raising us by herself because my father was in America working to make money for our growing family. When I was five years old, my father decided to bring his family to the United States to find a better life for us. One night in September, we left our home and took a train to Tijuana, a border town between Mexico and the United States. After a couple of nights of waiting to cross, we hiked our way through the mountains that bordered Mexico and California. The trek was not easy, but we made it to Los Angeles with the help of relatives who took us into their homes until we found a place of our own. We moved into an apartment where I shared a room with my sisters while my brothers slept in the living room. A couple of years later my mother gave birth to another sister and then another brother a year after that, making it more crowded in our tiny apartment. We moved to a slightly bigger house with a yard and, after a couple more moves, my parents were finally able to afford a house to call our own. My mother didn't work because she was too busy raising us. Much of this was achieved with the help of my older brothers and sisters who, instead of going to college, went to work to help my father pay the mortgage. As time went by, my older brothers and sisters got married and left home, leaving the younger ones to help out with the house expenses.

I wanted to go to college after graduating from high school and wondered how I could afford it and still help out with the family finances as my siblings had done in the past. Before graduating from high school, I took on a full-time job working at a clothing store in the afternoons, and on the weekends I helped my older sisters in their jobs to earn a bit more money for my college fund. Once I graduated from high school, I continued to work while taking courses at CSUN. I worked late nights, doing schoolwork during breaks, lunch, and on my way home on the bus or late into the night. A couple years later, my father was promoted to head baker at the bakery he worked for and didn't need as much help from us. I stopped working with my sisters, but I was still able to save money for school from my retail job. Later, I was promoted to assistant manager and got recruited to a retail box store.

Schoolwork was my priority until about two years ago when my father got laid off from work because the bakery was closed down due to the recession. My parents had never talked about money issues while I was growing up. Even after being laid off, my father kept a strong front by keeping any financial problems from the rest of us. Since my older siblings moved out, I had taken over the responsibility of checking mail correspondence in my family, sorting out and translating mail for my parents. Looking through the mail, I found out that my father had been taking money out of his retirement fund. He did not want us to find out about his financial trouble, fearing that we might give up school to help him out, so he asked his friend to help him fill out the paperwork to take out his retirement fund. It was very upsetting to find out that he had gone to such an extreme to keep his financial difficulty from us, but after I let my anger subside I had my mother call a family meeting to discuss the situation in order to find a solution.

The whole family was at the meeting. Unfortunately, my older siblings could only offer moral support since they now had their own families to take care of. We talked for hours, throwing ideas back and forth to figure out how we could fix our problem. We all agreed that my father had to stop withdrawing money from his retirement fund and also that my sister and I should finish the current semester in college but would take a leave of absence for the next semester. At that time, my twin sister and I were the only ones working in the family while my younger brother and sister were high school students. So we would have to figure out how to make ends meet. My twin sister had been going to CSUN, too, and working at one of the Target stores in the area. She would see if she could pick up more hours to get more money flowing into our account. I decided to take a promotion that I had been putting off because of school to get an increase in my salary. With my promotion came longer hours and more responsibilities at work, leaving me little time to even think of going to school. It was a sacrifice that I had to make for my parents since they had always worked so hard to give us a good home. My sister and I refused to let our parents lose the house after all the hard work they had put into getting their own little piece of the American Dream.

As it turned out, one of my older sisters was struggling to pay for her apartment after going through a divorce. Her work had also gone through a recent downsizing and, even though she did not lose her job, her hours were reduced to a part-time job. We all decided that it would work in our favor if she and her kids moved back into the house until the economy got better. Her moving back would be another source of income coming into the house to help us with the bills and also help her save some money to get back on her feet. The house became full again, but at least we were able to save it from foreclosure with all of us chipping in to pay the bills.

My father was having a hard time finding another job because people were not willing to hire an old person in their bakery. He reached out to other family members to see if any of them had leads on available jobs. When nothing came up, he decided to go back to gardening houses, something he had done on the side while working for the bakery. One of his friends had a list of customers for whom he worked, and he hired my father to take over some of the customers with his own crew. It was not a greatly profitable job, but at least it was something to keep him feeling like he was helping out at home. As he worked several houses, he started to get more referrals to other houses, making friends here and there with the owners of the houses. One day he was asked to be the head landscaper to one of the mansions he had worked for in Encino Hills. This job gave him more stability and made him feel more like the man of the house, which allowed him to begin to feel like his old self and less stressed around the house. Aside from doing this job Monday through Friday, my father has also kept some of the other houses on the weekends, wanting to put more money back into his retirement fund.

It has been a stressful year so far, with mother worrying about the money flowing in, even though she was not the one taking care of the account. She would look over my shoulder, making sure that all the bills were paid before letting us go out to spend on other things. In a way it felt like the old days when we were living in the apartment at the beginning of our lives in America, when she was really tight with our money. It has been a hard transition for my older sister, who was used to making her own money and spending it as she pleased, but under my parents' roof she had to follow their rules if she wanted to stay and save her money. It was not easy for me to get used to having a noisy, crowded house. Moreover, I was worrying about the semesters passing by and wanting to be back in the classroom to finish my degree. I would stay up late, losing sleep, hoping it would not be too long before we could get our household back to normal so I could go back to school. The only ones who did not seem to be affected by the change were my younger brother and sister; they continued to go to school as usual, with their grades staying in their usual A's and B's.

In recent months, it has finally started to feel like we can go back to the lives we were living before the recession. My parents flew to Mexico and sold some property that they owned over there and put some of the money into my father's retirement fund in hopes of getting it back to the balance it had before he withdrew out of it. When my father took out the withdrawals from his retirement fund he didn't realize that he was going to be charged a penalty for early withdrawal. Now, he is trying to pay that back, too. Hopefully, he learned his lesson to leave his retirement fund alone. Recently, my parents opened an emergency savings account in which they can put whatever extra money they may have accrued. We all decided that the account could not be touched without the consent of everyone living in the house. My older sister and her kids will be staying with us a bit longer, but she has begun to talk about moving out in the following year, and possibly moving into a studio apartment. I have postponed going to school this year, but I have started saving up to go back in the next fall semester, maybe taking a few courses in the beginning before taking on a full load. It feels like we have been through a lot of complications in the past two years, but I am sure that it could have been worse if we didn't have such a strong family bond. We will move forward and stay afloat in these tough times with the support of my older siblings and my parents' perseverance, strength, and hard work.

4

Intergenerational Refugee Resilience

Yvonne Kwan

Twenty-eight years ago, my husband's father, Chhourn Mak, escaped death and starvation from the Khmer Rouge. Due to the wars in Southeast Asia, Chhourn sought asylum in the United States in 1982 during the second wave[17] of refugee relocation. After Pol Pot gained power, my father-in-law and his family were forced out of their homes in the city to work in the rural rice fields. Chhourn details this experience:

> *A lot of people grew rice. They didn't let anybody go to school or go to work. When the communist control, they said everybody had to work in farm. They sent a lot of people out of town. Some people wanted to stay in town, they killed them. Even if you had a beautiful home, beautiful house or car whatever. You had to give it to them. And you just left your home. The whole Cambodia worked in farm.*

[17] The first wave of refugees out of Southeast Asia consisted of the educated and well-off individuals who were able to get access out of Cambodia before the Khmer Rouge takeover. The second wave of refugees came after the Refugee Act of 1980. According to Khatharya Um (1999:264), "In comparison with the smaller group of refugees who were resettled in 1975, the overwhelming majority of the later arrivals were less educated, more rural in origin, and generally less endowed with the skills, or the 'human capital,' that are generally deemed essential for successful resettlement."

Labor camps arose as Khmer Rouge soldiers deurbanized cities like Pursat, Battambang, and Phenom Penh. Aihwa Ong (2003:42) writes, "The Khmer Rouge turned the entire country into a series of labor camps and peasant cooperatives." Frequently, individuals in the labor camps were overworked, starved, and/or executed because they were supposedly having "political ties" that were against the communist regime of the Khmer Rouge. Under these repressive conditions, my husband's family fled Cambodia for Khao-I-Dang refugee camp at the Thai border. After a tedious resettlement process, Chhourn sought asylum in the United States.

Chhourn met his wife, Maly Phon, after resettling in Los Angeles. Maly was orphaned by the war in Cambodia. With few to no close family members, she married Chhourn and started a family at the age of seventeen. Chhourn and Maly have two boys. My husband, Brian Ung, was born in 1985. My brother-in-law, Ralph Prum,[18] was born in 1991.

Life was never easy, even after the escape from the Khmer Rouge. Chhourn vented about his situation: "In my country, when you work, you can feed the whole family. Here one person works and can only feed himself. So it's very hard. You feel upset about your job. In this country, you open your eyes you go to work and you come back and sleep. It looks like there's no freedom." Due to the recent economic downturn, Chhourn and his family plan to sell their home in order to have enough capital to start a business. He wants to start a business to establish job security. This is extremely risky because of the high failure rates of immigrant entrepreneurship. Like many Khmer Americans, Chhourn is a baker at a donut shop. His current employer is selling the business because the business is not as profitable anymore. Chhourn is afraid that he will lose his job when his employer sells the business. Maly does not work, so if Chhourn loses his job, they will lose everything. In order to secure employment, Chhourn has decided to buy the business from his employer. But with no capital, Chhourn must sacrifice their home.

With little skills, Chhourn believes he has no other choice during this economic recession. Chhourn will rely on his family to get the business started. Chhourn's work ethic and extensive family support help him and his family stay

---

[18] Each of the family members have different surnames because Chhourn says, "For us name is not very important." Ung is Chhourn's father's surname while Prum is Maly's grandfather's surname. Chhourn's name is actually not his real name. He changed it at the refugee camps due to the fear of persecution by the Khmer Rouge who might be able to track down his family name. According to Chhourn, as long as the family is together, name does not matter. However, a name is not just a word. A name has memory, history, and meaning. When Chhourn changed his name in order to protect his family from persecution, he was reborn into a different identity.

resilient under these hard economic times. Chhourn and his family are particularly resilient because they have already experienced extreme grief and loss. These hard times are nothing compared to the fear they experienced fleeing for their lives during the genocide in Cambodia. They are optimistic because they know that life now is still much better than life in Cambodia. Immigrants and refugees have the knowledge and strategies for coping with economic recessions because they have already learned to survive much tougher conditions. It almost seems like they are desensitized to hardship. When you have nothing to begin with, there is nothing you can lose.

Although the older generation has these prior experiences and strategies to cope with loss and pain, the younger generations often do not share this knowledge. The younger generations, however, learn to negotiate between their parents' past and their own present in unique ways. The Great Recession affects the second generation in a much different way than their parents. Brian and Ralph did not experience war or trauma in Cambodia, but they have learned strategies to cope with uncertainties growing up as children of refugees in the United States. Because Brian is the first-born and is older than Ralph, Brian has developed more effective strategies for coping with the recession. Ralph is a senior in high school, so he is still sheltered from the current economic woes. Brian, however, has different circumstances where he must navigate the changing times for his parents as well as for himself.

As the first person to attend college in his entire extended family, Brian had little cultural, economic, or symbolic capital (Bourdieu 1982). Because of this, Brian has had a tough time completing his undergraduate education. When Brian graduated high school in 2003, he was planning to attend California State University, Fullerton. But due to his lack of cultural capital, he did not realize that he needed to submit a "SIR (Student Intent to Register)." As a result of this, CSU Fullerton revoked his admission during the fall of 2003. Brian decided to enroll at Mt. San Antonio Community College (Mt. Sac). But with little emotional or economic support from his parents, Chhourn and Maly, he struggled. Many enter Mt. Sac, but few actually graduate or transfer. Brian finally transferred to Cal Poly Pomona in 2008 after five years at Mt. Sac. That was when the recession began. Because of the budget cuts imposed by the State of California, Brian struggles to enroll in the classes he needs to graduate. He is ready to finish his undergraduate degree in animal science, but the lack of courses offered is prolonging his already extended undergraduate education.

During summer (re)session of 2009, Cal Poly Pomona cancelled all summer school courses due to the budget cuts. Brian was originally enrolled in three courses, but was later dropped from all three courses due to the lack of funding from the state. To make matters worse, the required courses for his major were further curtailed during the academic school year. Brian waitlisted for a required lab course for three quarters before successfully enrolling in the course in spring quarter of 2010. In order to compensate for the cancelled courses in the summer, Brian averages nineteen units a quarter to try to catch up. Spring commencement 2010 is coming up, but Brian still cannot graduate. He has eight more courses to complete before finishing up his degree. He plans to complete these courses during summer session 2010 and fall quarter 2010, but financial aid is abysmal for "fifth" year (which is actually his "eighth" year) students. Brian will have to take loans to pay for all of his registration fees. In the past, he received financial aid in the form of loans, grants, and scholarships, but this upcoming year, loans will be his only option.

While attending school full time, Brian works 25 to 30 hours (sometimes 40 hours if needed) a week at his job at United Parcel Services (UPS). He has worked at UPS for five years now. Brian works swing shift from around 5:00 pm to 1:00 am so that he can attend school during the day. With only few hours of sleep, Brian must attend school, complete his homework, and help his parents negotiate life as immigrants/refugees. Brian complains, "Nothing in my life goes right! Everyone wants some from me." Because he is the oldest, his parents expect him to translate and assist in all matters large or small. Despite Brian's work and school duties, he has to help his mother settle a jury summons that she failed to respond to a few years ago; he has to help his father with police reports and credit reports because his father's bank account was defrauded; he has to drive his little brother to the Long Beach Gay Pride Parade because his brother does not drive and their parents do not know that Ralph is gay; and much more. The economic recession has hit Brian particularly hard because it adds an extra burden in addition to his regular responsibilities as a child of refugee parents. But it is precisely because of his responsibilities as a child of refugee parents that he has stayed resilient during these times. Although he cannot rely on his parents for emotional or monetary support, he has friends and family, including me, his wife, who offer him additional support. As our own family, Brian and I have learned ways to cope with and stay resilient during this economic recession. We learned from our parents' struggles as immigrants and refugees in this country.

Brian and I are both still students. It seems that we will never earn enough money to make ends meet even though we are both educated. We constantly worry about job security and monthly bills. It has become more and more difficult to manage our finances with our dismal income. During these rough economic times, having a quality education and/or an advanced degree does not guarantee success or a stable, well-paying job. The instabilities of the current times generate anxiety, stress, and depression, but both Brian and I know that it could be worse. We did not physically experience our parents' traumas, but their past continues to haunt us in a way that helps us understand and know their pain and experiences (Gordon 1997). The haunting becomes productive and informative.

Coping methods of both the first and second generations reach beyond the individual and private sphere of the home. Because these hard times are widespread, a public feeling regarding resilience is generated among other immigrants, refugees, and their children. According to Ann Cvetkovich (2003), public feelings of trauma, despair, and hope can create collective action, whether it is through social movements and protests or even just family dinners. The past historical-material conditions of immigrants and refugees inform ways the first and second generations respond to current historical-material conditions.

References

Bourdieu, Pierre. *Language and Symbolic Power.* Ed. John B. Thompson. Cambridge, Mass: Harvard University Press, 1982.

Cvetkovich, Ann. *An Archive of Feelings: Trauma, Sexuality, and Lesbian Public Cultures.* Durham and London: Duke University Press, 2003.

Gordon, Avery. *Ghostly Matters: Haunting and the Sociological Imagination.* Minneapolis, MN: University of Minnesota Press, 2007.

Ong, Aihwa. *Buddha is Hiding: Refugees, Citizenship, the New America.* Berkeley and Los Angeles, CA: University of California Press, 2003.

Um, Khatharya. Scars of War: Educational Issues and Challenges for Cambodian American Students. In *Asian-American Education: Prospects and Challenges,* 263–284. Ed. C.C. Park & M.M. Chi. Wesport, CT: Greenwood Publishing Group, Inc., 1999.

5

History: Recognition of Ourselves

Daisy Le

History is important. Recognizing what we have done in the past is recognition of ourselves. By researching our past, we are learning how to go forward in our present life. I never really stop to take a good look around and acknowledge that I am a privileged university student and that I am a Vietnamese American. Occasionally, I find myself taking many things for granted like money, education, and most importantly my parents. It was their courageous efforts during the time when Vietnam was on the edge of self-destruction that enabled me to be where I am today. I strongly look up to my parents as great role models because their experiences as Vietnamese refugees inspire me to take on different challenges. It is my father's historical narrative that continually reminds me of my family's past and of how lucky we are even to have a roof over our heads. It is also through this history of my family that I find the willpower to conquer every task at hand and to move forward in pursuit of my personal and professional aspirations. His experience has taught me to be more focused and determined to achieve what I want out of life. The obstacles he faced as a refugee strengthened his values for family and education, which ultimately contributed to the shaping of my values. My father's life is just a glimpse into a part of Vietnam's history. His experience also sheds a different light on Asian American history.

My father, Mr. Xuoi Van Le, was born on February 6, 1946, and grew up in the capital of South Vietnam, Saigon. He joined the U.S. Navy Seals in 1964. In 1969, when the Vietnam War seemed hopeless, the United States slowly began to withdraw its troops. The last U.S. ground troops left Vietnam two months after a cease-fire was arranged in January 1973. Despite the treaty, fighting between North and South Vietnam resumed soon afterward, but this time around, the U.S. troops did not return. The war finally ended on April 30, 1975, when South Vietnam surrendered to North Vietnam.

Although the war ended in 1975, its effects did not cease for my father. A few months before the war ended, his ship was captured, and the Northern communists took everyone onboard as prisoners. Later, they were sent to a "re-education camp" where they were detained for many years under harsh conditions and constant threat of death. When my father was sent to re-education camp, his family and relatives lost all hope of ever seeing him again. Regardless of this disturbing setback, my mother (his wife-to-be at the time) did not lose hope and assured him that she would wait. My father spent eight years in prison before he was finally released in October 1983. As she promised, my mother waited patiently for the day of her fiancé's release so they could rejoice in harmony. No more than four months after he got out, my parents ran away together against the objection of my mother's family and became boat people in search of the opportunity to start their new life together. My father left Vietnam for his freedom, the safety of his wife, and the future of his children. He left because he wanted to flee the communist government that was taking over his beloved homeland.

My parents arrived in Indonesia seven months later with an estimated 125 other Vietnamese. Their life in the refugee camp was simple. The majority of the people in the camp worked together and helped one another. Gender roles were not a huge issue at camp. Both men and women alike offered help whenever and wherever it was needed. Besides the entire camp working together to clean out all the barracks and the surrounding campgrounds every Monday, refugees staying at the camp were neither mandated nor demanded to work in the resettlement camp. With no work mandate, my parents had time to start and maintain a little business of their own. My parents bought a little hut from a well-to-do owner who didn't want it anymore. Even though it was a discounted deal, money was still hard to come by. With help from a few of their close neighbors, my parents were finally able to gather enough collateral to pay for the little hut and soon after became the proud owners of a small grocery shop that served the 5,000 refugee residents on the island of Indonesia.

Despite stories of the squalid encampment of more than 5,000 refugees on the island of Indonesia, my parents found the refugee camp an endurable support system away from Vietnam. The refugee resettlement camp provided its "guests" with small portions of rice and sugar on a daily basis. This got my parents through their days, and that was all that mattered to them at the time. The life they had in the refugee resettlement camp was actually not that bad at all. Being a former Navy Seal member, my father was offered a position as one of the camp security officers. His main duties were to patrol the boundaries surrounding the campgrounds and to ensure that there was not any inner-camp thievery. It may not have been the most glamorous position around, but it helped my father pass the days and allowed him to earn and save some extra pocket cash. In addition to owning their small grocery shack, this was another rare opportunity my parents were presented with. Known as a former Navy Seal fighting for his country and now seen as a protecting figure for their community, my father was respected by many of the refugees in the camp. Along with this respect, it was not surprising that trust in this hard-working couple trailed right behind. This may not seem like much, but for my parents, who deemed honor and integrity as a must in life, it *was* enough. Being respected by others and being trusted with opportunities to provide for their community gave my parents a purpose to life.

While Indonesia was the island of opportunity for my parents, they continued to dream of and hope for greater opportunities elsewhere, particularly in America. He spent every day in the refugee resettlement camp hoping that he and his wife could finally start fresh in a land of opportunity—America. In 1983, they got a sponsor and came over to America.

As with many refugee families who started their new life in America, my parents' transition to American life was difficult primarily due to heavy financial burdens and cultural barriers. Having had to settle down in the Tenderloin District of San Francisco, they were confronted with issues of unemployment, unstable family life, crime, poverty and, perhaps most sadly, despair. My parents barely spoke English and had little to no assistance in accessing social and healthcare services. This did not, however, discourage my parents from instilling in me the importance of diligence and persistence. The Vietnamese proverb, "Co cong mai sat; co ngay nen kim" which means "a person who works hard and dedicates herself to any endeavors in life will likely succeed and accomplish her objectives," celebrates and legitimizes the important values that my parents taught me. The shift to the new rigors of acculturating into a completely new society, as well as the financial and emotional responsibilities related to caring for me and my sister, heavily strained them physically and mentally. However, my parents' knowledge and understanding of the world and the path they wanted to follow were clear. Interacting with fellow refugees living in similarly underserved communities helped my parents to develop a new political consciousness, and they began to see a connection between their prior struggles overseas and the struggles that they were experiencing now in the States.

My parents realized that education was not only the best way to prepare their children for a better life but also it will motivate children to claim ownership of their parents' refugee experience. Being raised in a traditional Vietnamese working class family, my parents encouraged the belief that the ethic of hard work and dedication to a job well done was more valuable than intelligence alone. Yes, education was important, but maintaining cultural ties to my community and giving back was heavily stressed. It was with the support of and the ability to progress alongside with other refugee community members that my parents were able to survive the war and to adjust to life in America. Their resilience and hard work culminated in both their daughters' completion of college. I understand now that our experience growing up, with all its ups and mostly downs, was a blessing in disguise. It instilled in me a strong work ethic and resilience that aided me in the creation of an environment that supported my own personal success and survival. If it were not for my parents' struggles and their ultimate decision to leave Vietnam in hopes of better opportunities for my sister and me, we would not be where we are today and pursuing the paths that we do.

My parents' stories of the past and their desire to return one day to their homeland powerfully influence my decision to succeed in academics and to pursue a career in Asian American public health and education. I am eager to be in a position to share the knowledge and skills that I gain through higher education with those who are in need to help improve their quality of life. It is my aspiration to help people like my parents, who care about their families and communities, but simply do not have the resources and information to provide help. At the moment, my ultimate goal is to return to Vietnam with my family and to be able to open and facilitate a health clinic serving underprivileged communities. I want to be able to bring to them the opportunity for knowledge and access and to give back to them all that I have been blessed with.

Of course, with my aspiration comes motivation and determination. Without my parents' consistent support and encouragement, I would not have the drive to do the things that I do. Education is further enhanced by experiences, whether it is of one's own or another's. My parents' involvement during my early childhood was through the historical stories that they told. By reminding me of my family's past through their experiences, my parents instill values that are critical to my development as an individual. This ongoing learning experience sets me up to better perform academically and socially. As a college student who is at the threshold of self-reliance and independence, I can readily say that their concerns over parenting, education, and socialization depict the reality that is, in whole or some part, relative to my life experience. If it were not for my father's historical narratives of my family's past, I would not have such a vivid understanding of the living situations during the Vietnam War. And on top of that, if it were not for my mother's constant reminders about their struggles arriving in the United States, I would not have the determination, motivation, and inspiration to succeed everyday at the things in which I am involved. It is my parents' experience and constant drive to educate my younger sister and me about our family's past that makes me proud to be the Vietnamese-American woman that I am today. From celebrating Lunar New Years by praying in a temple to wearing the traditional *ao dai* to school during culture week, I have grown prideful of my culture, heritage, and history.

6

Learning from My Parents' Struggles

Jane Shin

I sat down and thought about how my life would have been different if I was still in Korea with my family. I wondered what kind of environment I would be surrounded by. In Korea, my parents had a respectable background with great education and high-paying, stable jobs, with no worries of being laid off. I remember when I was in Korea—my parents provided me with everything I needed from expensive clothing to expensive meals. One time, we had a sports event at school, in which all the parents brought some food as a potluck. Usually, each family would bring small portions of food like drinks and cookies to contribute to the potluck. However, though my parents could not make it because of work, they sent my grandmother instead, and I remember my grandmother bringing so much food that it was more than enough for all of my classmates. She even brought toys for everybody. Although I was young, I knew that our family never had to worry about money, and that I had a stable family.

However, in retrospect, those days seem ephemeral. One day, my parents decided to go to the United States, thinking that I would be able to live a better life and pursue a much better education in the United States. The decision that my parents made was quite surprising for me, because I never thought about going to a foreign country and learning a different language and getting a completely different type of education. Although I had lived in Japan when I was younger, it was more for the purpose of visiting for a while, rather than for the purpose of staying. My time in Japan was remembered as a time of relaxation. However, moving to the United States was a bit different, and it has changed my whole life in order to receive a different education. In Korea, English was and is considered to be a very important language that one must learn, so my parents probably felt that learning English in the United States would be better for me since I can obtain first-hand English experience among Americans.

This period was a turning point of my life, and I had mixed feelings about coming to the United States. On one hand, the radical changes in my life and new experiences excited me. On the other hand, I was very upset and afraid of the fact that I could no longer be with my friends that I had known for a long time in Korea. Because I was a rather introverted, timid person, I was worried that I may not be able to make any friends or fit in well in an American school. As multitudes of mixed thoughts and feelings filled my head, I slowly fell asleep in the plane, and by the time I opened my eyes, I had already arrived in the United States.

At first, ironically, this so-called "Land of Opportunities" did not provide opportunities for my family, but hardship. My parents had to sacrifice all the luxuries of a title, stable jobs, and wealth in Korea and had to start anew from scratch without any knowledge of this country, without any help, and without knowing English—all for the sake of a better education and a better life for me. I think that this was the first time I really began to feel a sense of burden and responsibility for my life, along with fear about uncertainty of the future and the possibility of disappointing my parents. However, my parents were always there to cheer me up and support me, although they had to bear their own hardship and burden. I think that I was able to get to the point where I am now because, even during times of adversity, of working in unfamiliar jobs, and weariness, my parents worked hard and supported me with everything they had.

The first couple years in the United States were the worst years of my life. When I first came to the United States, my mother and I came together, about one year later my dad joined us, because my dad had a problem with his visa. It was hard for my mother to find a new job here, and we had to support our family with the money that my father sent us from Korea. Our family faced huge financial burdens, and it got so bad that I could only eat about two meals a day at one point. But most of all, it was very difficult for me to go to a school where I could not communicate with anybody. I wanted someone I could talk to with ease; I wanted to see my dad who was in Korea, and I wanted to see all my friends that I had left behind. I cried so much at home and my eyes were swollen every day.

During that time, there was an instance that I cannot forget to this day. Because I couldn't speak English, I could not finish my school assignments. I wanted to ask my friends for help, but I did not have any friends at the time in my school. After not being able to turn in a number of assignments, I received a detention; I considered myself a hard-working student and this would have never have happened if I were in Korea. During my time as a student in Korea, I had the chance of becoming the class representative, and I loved to answer questions that teachers asked in class and help the teachers. It seemed as though the moment I got off the plane, I turned into a completely different person. I was unhappy with myself. I was failing academically and socially. I was appalled by the fact that I got a detention for not being able to do homework. Moreover, I ate alone during lunch time because I did not have any friends. I was afraid of myself and felt that I was turning into a problematic teenage girl who was completely helpless.

In order to overcome the language barriers, my mother and I carried an electronic dictionary in our bags to try to learn English. Whenever my mother and I needed to communicate with other people, we took out our electronic dictionaries and searched word-by-word to say what we needed. Others considered this as an oddity; people always gave us peculiar looks when we took out our dictionaries to find words we did not know.

After one year of such struggles, my dad finally came from Korea. When he arrived in the United States and saw how my mother and I were living, his expression became stiff, and he had the saddest look on his face. He realized how difficult a time we were having after seeing that we lived in a house that was smaller than the house we had in Korea. There were some dishes that my mom and I forgot to wash and put away, because we were so busy, and even this saddened my father. Immediately, my dad looked for a job in America, but there were not many jobs for him. By this time, it felt as though my family was no longer "normal" or even "stable," as we were in Korea. We always had to worry about money and everybody was on edge, even at home. We had learned to think twice about spending even a single dollar and saved as much as we could. Thankfully, my dad eventually found a job despite these difficulties. Although it was a job that was hard labor, he always told me that he was thankful for it. However, I always imagined how hard it must have been for him to work at such a low-end job that he was not used to, as a laborer. After a while, I could see the calluses and the bruise marks on my dad's hands, and, likewise, I could see that my mother was full of fatigue. Seeing my parents work so hard for me gave me a feeling that I could not express in words. Perhaps it was a mixed feeling of thankfulness and sadness. Nevertheless, I felt more and more that I had to be a daughter that my parents could be proud of.

It was finally time for me to choose the college I wanted to go to. However, it was difficult for my family to support my schooling. My dad could not pay for the school costs, even though he worked so hard, especially because as the economy slowed, he made an agreement to be paid less for a while. However, I got financial aid in college and could get an education. Nonetheless, my parents worked hard day and night and promised me that they would save enough money to help me continue on to graduate school. My parents have always told me that they will try to support me as much as they can for graduate school, and they always encourage me to go on. Hopefully, these economic issues get solved and things get easier so I can work after graduating from college. Seeing my parents work so hard just for me made me realize how much they love me. It is amazing to see that their sole motivation for working so hard and coping with financial problems during these hard economic times was to see me go to a good college. My experiences thus far in the United States have made me realize that there will always be hard times in life, no matter what. But my parents' actions give me the strength to overcome any obstacles in life.

SECTION 2

The Role of Institutional Support in Shaping Immigrant Resilience

Tracy Lachica Buenavista

Inherent in the public discourse on The Great Recession is the relationship between the dearth of public resources and the subsequent criminalization of those people accused of its decline. Despite the billions of dollars that immigrants and their families contribute in the form of taxes, they are often scapegoated as facilitating economic imbalance through an assumed overreliance on federal, state, and local resources.[1] As a result, during economic crisis, restrictions on eligibility for social services and other types of institutional aid often occur to quell anti-immigrant sentiment and movements that place the burden of public assistance on immigrants.[2] However, often fundamental to the survival and success of immigrants and other socially disadvantaged populations is the commitment by federal, state, and local entities to provide institutional support in the form of policies, programs, and services that attempt to curb social disparities. In this section, we reveal the ways in which resilience was shaped in part by the ability of students from immigrant families to access institutional support.

---

[1] The Immigration Policy Center released data indicating that undocumented immigrant households paid approximately 11.2 million in state and local taxes in 2010. The data is available at: http://immigrationpolicy.org/sites/default/files/docs/Tax_Contributions_by_Unauthorized_Immigrants_041811.pdf

[2] Lynn Fujiwara, *Mothers Without Citizenship: Asian Immigrant Families and the Consequences of Welfare Reform* (Minneapolis, MN: University of Minnesota Press, 2008).

Nativist Racism

In the words of critical legal scholar Robert S. Chang, "present-day nativism is grounded in racism."[3] Nativist racism is a social system that reflects a racially hostile, anti-immigrant sentiment and discourse that asserts "white nativist entitlement, rights, and belonging" in the United States.[4] During times of economic crisis, nativist racism increases to detrimentally shape immigration reform, as well as other policies that serve immigrant communities.[5,6]

Immigrants are often prevented from public assistance through the revision of policies that deem, or attempt to deem, naturalized citizenship as a criteria for institutional aid and program eligibility.[7] For example, although they are entitled to attend higher education, undocumented immigrant students—the majority of whom are people of color—are ineligible for federal and state financial aid.[8] Further, there have been increased restrictions on welfare eligibility and the difficulty for immigrants to access resources, such as public assistance, worsens disparities often facilitated by institutional barriers to aid.[9]

Such phenomena reflect a persistent trend for education and welfare reform to disproportionately affect immigrant communities of color. The relationship between the economic crisis and nativist racism shapes the context of the counter-storytelling in which students are engaged. As ethnic and racial minorities, their stories of resilience center on the availability of state-sponsored resources afforded to their immigrant families, as well as the difficulties involved in greater access to such institutional support. Different than individual characteristics and family support networks, resilience as mediated by institutional support reflects the social structures in which immigrant families operate. That is, institutional support or lack thereof is a manifestation of the larger societal sentiment that shapes the everyday lives of the immigrant families represented in this chapter.

---

[3] Robert S. Chang, "Toward an Asian American Legal Scholarship: Critical Race Theory, Post-Structuralism, and Narrative Space," *California Law Review* 81, no. 5 (1993): 1256.

[4] Fujiwara, 6.

[5] Douglas S. Massey, "International Migration at the Dawn of the Twenty-First Century: The Role of the State," *Population and Development Review* 25, no. 2 (1999): 303–322.

[6] Laura Pulido, "Immigration Politics and Motherhood," *Amerasia Journal* 35, no. 1 (2009): 169–178.

[7] Wendy Zimmerman and Karen C. Tumlin, *Patchwork Policies: State Assistance for Immigrants under Welfare Reform* (Washington, DC: The Urban Institute, 1999).

[8] Roberto G. Gonzalez, *Young Lives on Hold: The College Dream of Undocumented Students* (Washington, DC: College Board, 2009).

[9] Fujiwara.

Institutional Support

Institutional support comes in multiple forms. We use the term broadly to reference how immigrant families were able to rely on state and local institutions with pre-established mechanisms to access resources, both tangible and intangible, which were necessary to cope during difficult times. More specifically, we show how students from immigrant families rely on institutional support such as financial aid, campus work opportunities, social services, and public assistance to cope with struggles associated with The Great Recession. In doing so, we demonstrate more than the power for institution-sponsored resources to assist immigrant families; we also highlight the challenges and difficulties associated with the absence of, as well as access to, such support.

The ability for immigrant families to rely on these forms of assistance is especially important to consider because of the constant threat of these programs and services being reduced during periods of economic instability. A prevalent theme in the counter-stories is the impact of state budget cuts on public higher education, including the reduction of course offerings and financial aid. Students express a direct relationship between college enrollment, financial aid, work opportunities, and the way in which each factor shapes their resilience. In California, the economic recession is perhaps most marked by the restructuring of the higher education system to move from a state-sponsored funding model to one in which the burden of cost is placed on the families and students. While funding for institutions of higher education has been drastically cut, students simultaneously experienced a dramatic increase in their registration and other school-related fees. From 2005 until present, the percentage of state funding allocated to California higher education declined from 11.5 percent to 10 percent, a drop of approximately $1 billion.[10] As a result, the burden of college costs shifted to students and families. For example, during the same time period, the cost within the California State University system almost doubled from approximately $2,500 in 2005–06 to more than $4,400 in 2010–11.[11]

---

[10] According to the California State Budget 2005–2006, the total spending for higher education was $13.5 billion out of a total budget of $117.4 billion. This was higher than the total allocation for higher education in the California State Budget 2010–2011, which was $12.6 billion out of a total budget of $125.3 billion. Complete California state budget reports by year can be accessed at http://www.dof.ca.gov/budget/historical/2011-12/.

[11] Teri Yamada, "Restructuring the California State University: A Call to Action," *Thought & Action* 26 (2010): 91–106.

In California, not only have there been cuts to public education, there has also been decreased state spending on health care, elderly, and disability services.[12] For example, California cut funding for Healthy Families, a program that reduced healthcare costs for low-income families. Further, most if not all funding has been eliminated for services supporting maternal and adolescent health, HIV/AIDS patients, and domestic violence survivors. In this chapter, students' narratives greatly reflect the relationship between economic instability and other social disparities, including access to mental healthcare and public assistance.

Institutional Aid, Policies, and Services

Not to be lost in the students' depiction of financial and social hardship are the ways in which students' access to institutional support is used to navigate the relationship between hardship and immigrant family resilience. In other words, while students paint a picture of difficult social contexts, they do so only to assert the ways in which they seek resources to transform their situations. Students, while acknowledging how familial practices influence their academic and personal achievements, also implicitly show the limitations of self-reliance and the necessity of different forms of institutional support.

In the first story, Roza Chirishyan, an Armenian immigrant, shares how financial literacy, financial aid, and institutional programs historically shaped the educational opportunities for her and her family. Initially she describes her father's ability to create a savings plan that would provide an economic foundation on which her family could build their lives in the United States. The financial literacy he passed onto Roza included not spending beyond their means and placing limitations on the amount of debt one would accrue. Further, more significant was Roza's account of her mother's ability to learn English and enroll Roza and her sister in a daycare program at a local community college when they were children. She attributes the availability of affordable educational opportunities coupled with financial aid as a form of institutional support that ultimately modeled the potential for education to provide the resources for her family's eventual economic security.

Similarly, in the second story, Abraham Rodriguez, the son of Latino immigrants, discusses the relationship between college enrollment, financial aid, and the socioeconomic well-being of his family. Abraham's narrative begins with a depiction of the burden many California State University college students experienced

---

[12] Nicholas Johnson, Phil Oliff, and Erica Williams. *An Update on State Budget Cuts: At Least 46 States Have Imposed Cuts that Hurt Vulnerable Residents and Cause Job Loss* (Washington, DC: Center on Budget and Policy Priorities, 2011).

immediately after the rise in registration fees and reduction in course offerings—to qualify for financial aid, students scrambled to enroll in the minimum twelve units of coursework. However, because of the limited number of courses being offered, students were often forced to enroll in courses that: 1) did not progress them towards graduation, and 2) were scheduled during times that disrupted one's ability to work a traditionally scheduled job. Abraham describes how he struggled to balance two jobs and full-time enrollment, but also how his eligibility for federal financial aid enabled his family to stay afloat during the economic crisis. Abraham's story is important because he highlights how institutional limitations can have a trickle-down effect on student retention and employment, and in doing so encourages readers to understand the intimate link between class enrollment and financial aid eligibility, as well as the impact of enrollment on immediate work opportunities.

While Roza and Abraham's stories emphasize the role of financial aid on educational opportunity, Julie Tran's story provides insight regarding the importance of campus work opportunities. Julie, a second-generation Vietnamese American and first-generation college student, explains how her involvement as a peer mentor in a campus-sponsored program helped her to remain resilient in both school and family contexts. She was able to find an extracurricular activity that provided a stipend, which enabled her to remain on campus and contribute to funding her education. The educational stipend she received helped to designate her other income to her family's well-being. Like Abraham, she recognizes the delicate relationship between retention and employment for working students, yet her story exemplifies how institutional support in the form of campus employment contributed to her academic success.

It is important to note that Roza, Abraham, and Julie all relied on institutional support provided through federal financial aid and state funding for higher education programs promoting student retention. However, what happens when students are not eligible for such support? The question of eligibility is central to understanding Raymundo Hernández' narrative. Raymundo, an undocumented Mexican immigrant and accomplished community-based artist, uses his experiences to show the barriers that many undocumented immigrant youth face in California and throughout the United States. He describes how he and other undocumented immigrant youth fight an uphill battle to pursue higher education. Although he details the great lengths he goes to find work, cut costs, and save his money, his ability to go to college, and eventually graduate school, is dependent on California Assembly Bill 540, a state policy that grants some youth eligibility for in-state tuition.[13] Thus, one of the biggest contributions of

[13] For more information regarding AB540, please see: http://www.ab540.com/

Raymundo's narrative is the analysis that structural change is needed to assist in the resilience of students from immigrant families.

While the first four stories focus on the central role of financial aid and college costs, Hansook Oh charges readers to look at the other ways in which institutions of higher education can provide support. Hansook, a second-generation Korean undergraduate and student activist, reveals how the resilience she and her family have is due in part to the mental health services often afforded to students. She bravely shares her story of the compounding effects of poverty and depression and points to the availability of counseling services in colleges as one mechanism to seek support. It is important to note that, although she tells her story to show how such institutional support can contribute to one's resilience, Hansook forces readers to ponder what happens to healthcare access for the majority of people who are not able to attend college.

The concluding story of this chapter is by Robert Beam, who challenges readers to examine institutional support beyond a higher education context. Robert, a multiracial American who is married to a Japanese national, provides an important perspective not always considered in examining the impact of the economic crisis on immigrant families: public assistance. His discussion on the centrality of welfare in many families' experiences demonstrates the necessity to interrogate the role of public assistance in shaping resilience. In his story, Robert recounts both the struggles and perseverance that he and his partner experienced in accessing public assistance, namely the California food stamp program. As a full-time student, husband, and new father, Robert represents many non-traditional students attempting to attain a college degree while balancing family needs. In his story, he details the numerous efforts he and his partner made to find stable employment, as well as the economic circumstances that ultimately made public assistance unavoidable. In doing so, he poignantly communicates the significance of state public assistance programs in contributing to the resilience of immigrant families, including those who are of mixed status.

The Relationship Between Resources and Resilience

In all of the stories, the students believe that their individual well-being is inextricably linked to the resiliency of a larger collective, namely their families. Such ways of thinking explain the great length to which students will go to access institutional support to create better conditions for those immediately around them. Also inherent in their narratives is a central critique of the accessibility to various forms of institutional support. While they all intend to demonstrate how institutional support is central to their resilience, they are all aware of the inability for many others to be eligible, obtain, and/or be informed about different forms of institutional support. In the latter three stories, they also discuss the stigma attached to undocumented immigration, mental health, and public assistance, which complicates access to institutional support. Thus, while the resilience of immigrant families during The Great Recession must be understood experientially, one must read the following counter-stories as symptomatic of larger structural issues that disproportionately position immigrant families to fight an uphill battle to survive.

Bibliography

Fujiwara, Lynn. *Mothers without Citizenship: Asian Immigrant Families and the Consequences of Welfare Reform.* Minneapolis, MN: University of Minnesota Press, 2008.

Gonzalez, Roberto G. "Young Lives on Hold: The College Dream of Undocumented Students." Washington, DC: College Board, 2009.

Johnson, Nicholas, Phil Oliff, and Erica Williams. "An Update on State Budget Cuts: At Least 46 States Have Imposed Cuts that Hurt Vulnerable Residents and Cause Job Loss." Washington, DC: Center on Budget and Policy Priorities, 2011.

Massey, Douglas S. "International Migration at the Dawn of the Twenty-First Century: The Role of the State." *Population and Development Review* 25, no. 2 (1999): 303–322.

Pulido, Laura. "Immigration Politics and Motherhood." *Amerasia Journal* 35, no. 1 (2009): 169–178.

Yamada, Teri. "Restructuring the California State University: A Call to Action." *Thought & Action* 26 (2010): 91–106.

Zimmerman, Wendy, and Karen C. Tumlin. "Patchwork Policies: State Assistance for Immigrants under Welfare Reform." Washington, DC: The Urban Institute, 1999.

7

Creating a Legacy of Financial Literacy: Savings Practices and Financial Aid

Roza Chirishyan

Sometimes life brings unexpected circumstances in peoples' lives that come with dramatic changes, such as moving from one country to another. Individuals who travel and live in different cities and states sometimes experience culture shock. Imagine coming from a different country with a different language, different religion, and different traditions.

My family and I moved to the United States from Armenia in 1991, when I was four years old. At that time we were a family of four—my parents and my sister who was three at the time. My dad, grandfather, and uncle all had average, middle-class paying jobs in Armenia up until the great earthquake of 1988. An earth-shattering earthquake hit the city of Lenninakan that destroyed the entire city and killed and wounded many. Nothing was the same after the earthquake. Luckily, we had relatives in another city in Armenia that were not as impacted by this disaster; we moved in with them temporarily so that my family would have some time to recuperate.

The government did not give its citizens the help they desperately needed, so we were left to struggle until we could find a way out. My mother had relatives who lived in the United States; in Los Angeles. She wrote them a letter, we borrowed money, and in a few months we moved to "the land of opportunity" with debt and not a single dime in my father's pocket. Our relatives were kind enough to allow us to stay with them to get adjusted to this new country where we did not speak the language or understand the culture.

My mother often tells the story of how my sister and I cried for months to go back to our home, where most of our family was. She said we would cry and not sleep all night. We were kids and did not understand why we had to take the risk we did, but now looking back I am extremely grateful for the step my parents took. I now understand the decisions they made in order for us to have a better future.

Growing up, every day was a struggle for my dad to find a job that would enable us to move out of our relatives' home and pay off the debt we owed them. Finally, after several months of working temporarily for different employers, he found a full-time, permanent job, and we were able to move into an apartment and slowly begin paying off our debt. Our parents had to budget carefully to make ends meet. My dad always says, "It's not how much money you make; it's how you spend it." This is one of the great lessons I have learned from him and one that has been very useful for me. At one time he was only making $250.00 a week, but he and my mother managed to raise a family.

Even though we had debt and my dad was the only provider, he managed to put away a small amount each month to save in case of emergencies and for our future. Gradually, he paid off our debt and got a second and sometimes even a third job. He also set high goals to attain. Some of the goals included buying a house, going on a vacation together, and providing for us the best he could.

My dad, however, was not the only one working towards a better future. Los Angeles City College had the *Gain Program* and financial aid available. With both of these programs my mother was able to attend school and enroll my sister and me in a pre-school daycare. If it had not been for financial aid and grants for needy families, my mother would not have been able to attend college and take care of us at the same time. Due to these types of funding, my mother learned English, and my sister and I had the chance to experience pre-school daycare, which helped us develop our language abilities and got us ready for school.

As I was growing up, I learned that sacrifice and hard work could get you a long way. Unlike some of the practices that many Americans live by now, growing up I learned that you do not spend money you do not have. If you want something, you have to plan ahead and make sure that what you want does not interfere with or take away from your daily necessities. For example, if I have a $500 credit card bill, I will not add more on it. I will wait until that amount is paid off or dramatically decreased before I can make another purchase.

I also learned that we do not need many things to get by, but surprisingly we are a society that creates superficial needs and desires without really considering whether those things are really necessary. We do not need thirty pairs of jeans, but because we must be up-to-date with the trends and latest fashion out there, we buy more than we need. The media plays a great role during these tough economic times. Commercials advertise the latest cars, the newest trends, the biggest houses. Everyone wants to be accepted in her or his community, and it feels like everyone is in competition with one another: Who has the better car? Who is wearing the most expensive shoes? And the list goes on.

Growing up in my former neighborhood in Hollywood, California, all of my neighbors were the same way. They would buy the most expensive cars and park them in front of their apartment, while my family settled for what we could afford and saved for a better future. Currently, my family is the only family on that block who are about to become owners of a home because, at the time, we did not fill our apartment with unnecessary items, go on lavish vacations or bury ourselves in credit card debt. There are some unpredictable circumstances, such as losing a job, that are concerning many families in today's economic crisis, but how many families can make an effort to put money aside? I suspect that most likely the percentage of families that have the ability to do this is very small.

From looking at the financial struggles my family went through when we first moved to the United States, I have learned to save and spend accordingly. We never know what the future has in store for us. Putting away money for a time of distress will help somewhat ease the situation until we can stand up on our feet again. Parents can instill this type of behavior in their own kids at an early age in order for them to become aware of the bad consequences that buying on impulse or building debt can have on their lives. However, besides my parents' saving skills, I can't forget that the main reason we are where we are is due to the assistance we got from financial aid and grants that allowed us to get this far. Without financial aid and the grants made available, my mother would not have been able to get the education she received because there was no way to afford anything other than food and rent until my father's wages increased.

8

"La Vida": Coping with School, Work, and the Economic Crisis

Abraham Rodriguez

My name is Abraham Rodriguez, and I am a twenty-two-year-old man, born and raised in the United States. The current economic crisis has definitely had an impact on my life, especially on my education. Paying tuition has not been a big issue thanks to my eligibility to receive academic scholarships and governmental financial aid, but other necessities, such as books and school tools necessary to academically excel, have been financially difficult to get. Further, courses are being cut, and it has been difficult to get a seat in classes. Ultimately, this has affected my ability to graduate on time. I was not able to enroll in the appropriate classes this semester, and I had to take classes that meant nothing to me in order to fulfill my twelve unit semester qualification in order to continue receiving financial aid. This situation, which the school itself called an "economic crisis," resulted in an inconvenient class schedule that limited my work options.

As an employee of the city of Los Angeles, my hours were significantly cut down from thirty to ten hours a week because the city also had to deal with the budget crisis. I also have a second job, baking goods early in the morning, which is one of the only jobs I could find to accommodate my unordinary class schedule. I consider my family to be "lower-middle class"; my seventy-year-old father is retired and my mother cleans houses. My job with the city enabled me to provide some financial relief for my family, but since the reduction of my work hours, it has become financially tougher for our entire household.

The economic crisis has created a stressful situation with school, work, and family. The stress has taken a mental, physical, and emotional toll on me because there are more things to worry about. I began to wonder why I was going to school. There are so many people being laid off and looking for jobs, some in more desperate situations than my own. What will I do after college? With so many others unemployed, will there be job opportunities for me? Such questions have led to exhaustion, personal doubt, and even depression. I grew up with the idea that you go through school and if you work hard enough, you will graduate, find a stable job, get married, and raise a family. For me, it is too difficult to even think about getting married and raising a family of my own in the future, when currently this crisis has kept me from providing for my family and me.

Coping with the situation is difficult, but it is what my mom calls "la vida." I tend to look at my parents for support and ease. I take one look at them and I think to myself, if two immigrants, one from Mexico and another from El Salvador, can make it here, raise two kids and have them get through college, then I can do it too. My parents had close to nothing coming into the United States. I have many more advantages thanks to them. Another large form of support is a friend of my mom's for whom she has been cleaning for more than twenty years. This particular family has provided my family and me with both moral and financial support.

Spiritually, I find myself strong. I am currently a non-practicing Catholic. I went to church on and off all through middle school and high school considering they were private catholic schools. I found a lot of spiritual relief while in high school and now in college. I pray for strength, which helps calm me through such crises as the one we are currently in.

My family and I have not pursued any government help other than my financial aid for college and whatever financial help my parents get for my dad's social security benefits. Something is better than nothing. For me, family is the most significant tool towards getting through this crisis. The government is second in importance due to the huge financial support it has provided for me in the past five years of my college career. You'll have the occasional guardian angels, such as the extended family that has generously provided for us, too. There are wonderful people out there willing to lend a helping hand when they know that tough financial situations, as the one we are in, are not helping build up the community.

While in college, the Chicana/o studies courses I have taken have been reassuring to me as well. We discuss the current financial crisis, and it helps me realize that I am not alone. This crisis is affecting thousands to millions of all different ethnicities. It is our strength and resilience that will help us overcome this obstacle. I feel that we must adapt to the circumstances and be strong pulling out of this and any other crisis.

9

Working School: The Role of On-Campus Financial Opportunities

Julie Tran

My name is Julie Tran, and I am a second-generation Vietnamese American. In 1979, my parents came to the United States as refugees to escape the harsh social and political conditions in Vietnam after the Vietnam War. Their journey to and eventual lives in the United States were difficult, yet their resiliency literally and figuratively modeled the way in which I would approach my own journeys, particularly my pathway through higher education. From my parents' experiences, I saw the need to rely on multiple sources of support to achieve goals. Due to not only the support of my family and loved ones, but also the institutional support afforded to me by my education, I graduated with my bachelor's degree, went onto graduate school, and continue to use education and my access to institutional resources to remain resilient through both socioeconomically and emotionally difficult times. In this story, I focus on financial opportunities at school and how it helped both my family and me during hard economic times.

Upon arriving in the United States, my parents had little opportunity for socioeconomic mobility. Because they had not gone to college, their work options were limited. I quickly learned how low socioeconomic status had a toll on my access to school and even my family's overall health. My dad was the main financial provider while my mom worked part time and took care of my siblings and me. Our lack of financial stability caused my father a lot of stress, and one way he would attempt to cope with his troubles and sorrows associated with his refugee experience and our poverty was to turn to alcohol and cigarettes. Eventually, occasional drinking and smoking turned into an addiction that would lead to the deterioration of his health.

My dad's illness became so overwhelming that he had to stop working and my mom shifted to becoming the primary financial provider. Although she tried to remain physically healthy, our socioeconomic insecurity led her to constantly worry about how she was going to provide for our family. The stress led to sleepless nights, and the resulting exhaustion made her prone to physical illness. In response, as soon as I became eligible to work, I did, so that I could help my family with our finances.

I have worked since I was sixteen, so when I began college, there was no question of whether or not I would work, but rather, how much I would work. School became one way that I would escape from the stress at home, because people with similar struggles constantly surrounded me. At California State University, Northridge (CSUN), it was not rare to be a working student. Even more so, I was an Asian American studies major, part of a department in which many of the students were also low-income, first-generation college students. Most people I befriended received financial aid and also attempted to balance school with their family and work obligations. We would confide in each other about our academic and personal difficulties, but would also attempt to share with each other our strategies to overcome them. I felt that my struggles, as well as my success, were very much a collective one.

However, while being an Asian American studies major provided me a space to feel support, as important was the tangible financial opportunities I received through the department. In my last two years at CSUN, California went through severe economic times. Our fees increased while employment and financial aid opportunities decreased. I was working twenty hours a week at a low-paying retail job, and all my earnings were used to supplement my family income. However, when our fees increased, I needed to find another source of income that would not take away from the money I gave my family or be detrimental to my degree completion. With the help of department faculty, I learned of my eligibility to receive a stipend by working as a peer mentor.

CSUN's College of Humanities hosts the Peer Mentoring Program, in which the goal is to increase the retention rates of lower-division students. I was recruited to work with first- and second-year college students enrolled in a lower-division Asian American studies course. I was responsible for sharing with them time-management strategies, as well as academic and other campus resources. This campus job allowed me to work with my peers, develop communication and leadership skills, and create friendships. I would discuss with students the weekly readings, concerns about upcoming exams, and anything else regarding academics and personal issues. These interactions allowed me to expand my knowledge and helped me to develop the passion to become an educator.

It was important for me to have worked with the Peer Mentoring Program because it gave me the opportunity to not only work with my peers, but it also provided me additional financial assistance to support my enrollment at school. Although I continued to work my retail job, the additional aid I received at school helped not only with my retention but my family's financial health. My experience as a peer mentor was a productive outlet to simultaneously help other students, work on campus, stay focused on my studies, and assist my family during a really harsh economic period.

I learned that life sometimes is unpredictable, and it has its ups and downs, but we need a support system to help us to get through it. Although my friends and peers provided me the emotional support to cope with the stress of my parents' health complications and the struggle of balancing school and work, I believe students also need more options for tangible support, like campus employment opportunities. Work opportunities hosted and located at school allowed me to stay on campus so I could invest my time and energy on activities that supplemented my coursework, while also giving me a stipend I could use for funding my education. I believe that all students, but especially those who have been hardest hit by the economic crisis, could benefit from an increase in campus work-study opportunities.

10

The Struggles and Successes of an AB 540 Student: Fighting for Institutional Policy Reform in Higher Education

Raymundo M. Hernández

When we speak about undocumented immigration, we often focus on the experiences of undocumented immigrants who travel to the United States for better opportunities, freedom, and economic stability. Rarely are the experiences of "unauthorized" children documented or valued, although these children also carry stories of struggle and sacrifice. For this reason, I will share my story as an undocumented immigrant child and student and how the current economic crisis has affected the social, economic, and educational aspects of my life.

Currently, I am a twenty-eight-year-old graduate student at California State University, Northridge (CSUN). My journey to this place began when both of my parents made the decision to leave Mexico in the early 1990s to provide a better future for my sister and me in the United States. They wanted to pursue a higher standard of living not available to them in their home country. They knew that my sister and I would not be able to have a secure future if we stayed in México, and migrating to the United States was the only available option we had to gain social and economic mobility. As a boy, I never understood the concept of migrating to a new country, how it would affect my life in a positive or negative manner, or what obstacles I would encounter. I only understood what every eight-year-old kid could understand: games, cartoons, toys, and fun; all of which I left behind.

In the late eighties and early nineties, we lived in Amecameca, México, which is a small town forty-five minutes away from Mexico City. One day my parents informed us that we would be traveling to visit family. We were made to understand that the main purpose of our travel was to visit my maternal grandparents in Tijuana, Mexico, and attend an uncle's wedding, and then visit family in Los Angeles, California. After they shared the travel plans, we began to pack our home items into boxes, as if we were taking them with us. I looked forward to reuniting with my family, whom I had not seen in years. At the same time, seeing our house items stored away in boxes led to the fear that I would not be able to return.

In order to travel to Tijuana, Mexico, and the United States, my parents, sister, and I had to apply for a passport. It was a bureaucratic process, and I recall my mother carrying a large amount of paperwork with her, which contained proof of bills, income, home ownership, and anything that was needed to provide enough information. It took us at least one month from the day we first applied to the day we walked away holding our passports.

It is to my understanding that after the wedding, my uncles (my mother's brothers) tried to convince my parents to migrate to Los Angeles where we could pursue better opportunities and a better lifestyle. At first my parents were hesitant about the idea of permanently residing in the United States; therefore, there was a timeframe where we would travel back and forth from Tijuana to Los Angeles. After a while, my parents finally decided to stay in Los Angeles, but just long enough for my sister and me to learn the English language. Unfortunately the process of learning the language was a long process. Therefore, one year became two years, and two years became four years, until our temporary stay became permanent.

In the United States, our economic status was a major concern. My father worked two jobs a day making $4.25 an hour, the minimum wage in California at the time. We lived paycheck-to-paycheck, and our bills consumed most of my father's hard-earned money. Before coming to the United States, I envisioned a new world with less worry but unfortunately reality is cruel, and ever since I understood that our economic status would be limited. I admit that due to my poor economic status I learned to normalize our economic crisis as routine sacrifices.

I graduated high school in 2000, a time in which colleges and universities did not have any mechanism for serving undocumented youth. My undocumented status translated to a lack of access to financial aid, so I was limited to enrolling as a foreign student at the local community college, where I was forced to pay an enormous amount of tuition. In order to pursue my academic dream, I worked two minimum-wage jobs, saved all my earnings, and limited myself from participating in social events. I did not have a social life because my efforts went to school, studying, and working. A year into my community college experience, I fell into depression mainly because of my legal status and not having the opportunity to be like the "average" American student.

In 2002, a landmark bill was passed in California, Assembly Bill (AB) 540. AB 540 is a law that enables citizens, residents, and undocumented immigrant students who meet specific criteria to pay in-state fees at any California public college or university. I was qualified and became an AB 540 student, which alleviated my burden of paying out-of-state tuition as a foreign student. AB 540 made me feel that public higher education was more accessible to pursue, but I still faced difficulties.

I transferred to CSUN where I pursued a degree in art with an emphasis in graphic design. To save enough money to pay for my registration fees, books, art supplies, new computer, and food, I had to work three jobs. My parents also helped me to pay for groceries and rent. The financial and moral support from my parents helped me get through college and gave me the energy to continue to pursue higher education. I graduated in 2005, and through social networks was able to find a job. From this job I saved enough money to pursue graduate school. I began the Chicana/o studies graduate program at CSUN in 2006.

Similar to my undergraduate experience, I entered the graduate program as an AB 540 student with no financial aid, scholarship assistance, and/or resources for loans. Currently, I work full time and go to school part time. I am pursing a graduate degree because one day I intend to become a professor at a four-year university. Pursuing the degree in Chicana/o studies has allowed me to become more conscious about my community and politicized about contemporary immigration debates. Also, as an artist and scholar, I have found a way to connect the two professions by researching and creating critical political art in support of Comprehensive Immigration Reform (CIR) and the federal Development, Relief, and Education for Alien Minors (DREAM) Act. The Chicana/o studies curriculum, professors, and classmates play a central role in my ability to survive this current recession, because they have provided an institutional space in which I can come out of the shadows and open up to others regarding my legal situation.

Considering all the hurdles and obstacles in my life, AB 540 has made education more accessible. The law gives me temporary acceptance within this society by providing me the right to improve myself through educational attainment. If AB 540 had not made registration fees more reasonable, I never would have pursued an undergraduate degree and/or a graduate degree. When The Great Recession hit the United States, AB540 continued to be a law that helped me and many other undocumented students stay in school. However, as fees continue to rise, it is becoming increasingly difficult for undocumented students to attend and remain in school. Although I, as well as other undocumented students, face many uncertainties, we hope that institutional policies change to increase educational access and the potential to survive harsh economic times.

11

When Family Is Not Enough: Institutional Support as a Mechanism for Survival

Hansook Oh

My name is Hansook Oh. I am a second-generation Korean American, and currently I attend California State University, Northridge as a double major in journalism and Asian American studies. People who know me would probably describe me as a happy, confident, and ambitious person who does very well in school. I am proud to say that all of these things are true about the person I am today. However, most people do not know how hard I had to fight to live during the past two years and how different I would be today if I did not have access to the resources provided by higher education and other institutional support.

From my perspective, poor people are always in a recession. Thus, when the economy takes a big hit, it hurts pretty badly when your wallet is already near empty. I entered college in 2008, when the impact of the economic recession began to manifest itself throughout the country. Left and right, people were losing their jobs and homes, even in a city like Los Angeles, California, which is perceived to be lucrative. For some, it was the first time they faced this kind of trouble. For my family, however, financial instability was nothing new.

All our lives, my younger brother and I were used to having very limited resources and many disadvantages. For about ten years now, my family's annual income has been under $20,000, which according to federal standards translates into living below the poverty line. My father is a self-employed martial arts master and teaches Taekwondo for a living, and his business has not been doing well for a long time. My mother is unemployed due to an injury she sustained in 2003, although she could only find part-time work prior to her injury. To keep ourselves afloat, my parents have been digging themselves deeper and deeper into debt, using credit cards to pay the bills. Fortunately, our family did not lose our house, and my father was able to sustain several clients who were not greatly affected by the recession. We still felt the pinch and hated tightening up an already stringent budget.

Due to my family's financial status, when I entered college I was eligible for federal and state financial aid, which covered my registration fees and provided me enough funds to pay for books and other school-related necessities. I was also able to find a job tutoring youth, a job I held for about two years. The position paid me enough to cover gas, groceries, and other daily expenses. Everything seemed to be going okay during the first few months of college, though we did not have much. Starting school and finding a real job was exciting for me, and those two responsibilities were positive distractions from my depressing home life.

I use the word *depressing* because each of my family members suffers from some mental health condition, which no doubt is related to the stresses of poverty. For example, my mother suffers from post-traumatic stress disorder from previous hardships. My father, on the other hand, struggles with obsessive-compulsive disorder and anger management. As Korean immigrants, my parents never liked to admit that they had some unmet health needs, and at the same time, there were not really many services available that were sensitive to immigrant needs. Due to this situation, both my younger brother and I grew up learning not to be reliant on our parents for a "traditional" family experience. Further, when I was four I was sexually assaulted by a neighbor. My parents were not aware of the various services to which I was entitled, and as a result of this experience, I also suffered from post-traumatic stress disorder and terrible self-esteem. I grew up seriously depressed and struggled with suicidal and self-destructive thoughts on a daily basis.

As I grew older, I attempted to cope with my mental distress by becoming very involved with my church. I felt safer at church than I did at home and did not question the homophobic or anti-women ideals espoused by the church leaders. At the time, church was probably the only thing keeping me alive, and I did not want to lose that. However, when I began college I realized that although the church gave me some emotional support, I believed the lessons to be dogmatic, and my critical thinking and sense of self were stifled. I eventually left the church because I did not agree with its conservative ideals. Though I felt liberated by leaving, I also gave up the community to which I had deeply invested my time and energy. I had no other support system that could immediately replace the church, and I felt more alone and confused than ever.

Like many young people, I started to smoke and abuse painkillers in response to the bouts of depression and panic attacks I experienced. I wanted to quit my job and check into a rehabilitation facility, but I was constrained by the fact that my family and I literally could not afford to lose my income. I was left feeling helpless and hopeless—that is, until I found out that my school offered free counseling services to all students. I was ecstatic and got set up with a therapist who I ended up working with for eight months. During my time in therapy, I realized that I still suffered from my traumatic childhood experiences. With support, I worked through my issues and stopped using substances to cope. I also developed a strong sense of self and instead of being self-destructive, learned how to be sustainable in times of distress. Without such institutional support from school, I would not have been able to cope with the varying crises that enveloped my family.

If institutional support like funding for higher education and subsidized healthcare were not available to our family, I do not know what my life would have become. I would not be in school and would likely be using unhealthy ways to cope with depression. It is unfortunate that many people think subsidies to higher education and services to the poor are a waste of taxpayers' dollars. Because of the economic recession and California's billion-dollar debt, the governor has proposed to balance the budget by taking billions from higher education and social services like Medi-Cal and welfare-to-work programs. At the same time, the private sector is reluctant to invest in this stagnant economy, so jobs are scarce and growth is sluggish. The future of funding for public institutions in this state looks grim. People like me, who are already at a socioeconomic disadvantage, cannot afford to lose the little institutional support we have. If my support systems are threatened, my resiliency and well-being are also threatened. I could not have become the healthy, self-confident, and hard-working individual I am today if I did not have access to these resources. I am determined to be a person who makes a positive impact in my community and to give back to society, but I would not be able to be in the position of helping others if I had not received help for myself in the first place.

Sometimes family is not enough. I believe my parents were not able to be responsible for their children's well-being because historically they were not able to access the types of programs I am able to access today. Though I generally believe it is up to individuals in society to be responsible and accountable to their needs, funding for higher education and social services often serve as the mechanism for institutions to catch and address the needs of the many people who fall through the cracks. If we don't provide access to education and social services for all, our whole society will suffer the consequences in the long term.

12

Fighting through a Recession: The Relationship between Public Assistance and Resiliency

Robert Beam

In 2006, I married the love of my life. She was a Japanese national who did not come to the United States for economic freedom, but for love. Little did we know that in the following years the global economy would collapse, and our existence would depend on the efficiency and availability of government assistance. All of this was done in an attempt to move forward instead of spiraling backwards into debt.

My wife became a first generation Asian American in July of 2007. Her move to the United States was difficult. She missed anything and everything about Japan. She wanted to go back, she wanted to be able to see her family and friends, and she wanted to teach. It was her dream to teach Japanese, one she had been pursuing before she met me, but no one in the United States would hire her. Her degree from a Japanese college didn't equate to an American teaching credential. One of the hardest things for my wife, and something that she still struggles with today, is the language barrier. Although she speaks English very well, the inability for others to validate her ability has led her to be subconscious of her accent.

The economy really started to affect us in 2007, as I went into the second semester of my third year in college. My registration fees for the academic year increased as a result of the California budget crisis, and financial aid was only enough to directly cover academic costs. That semester, my wife and I lived on less than $200 a month. Our rent was covered from some assistance from family members, but utilities such as gas, electricity, and food were not. We took out credit cards, paid bills late, and I would work on the side building computers and selling them. Like many people in California, we sought out more work opportunities, but it was difficult. The unemployment rate in California at the time was 12%, but it was much higher for African Americans and immigrants. My wife eventually found a job working at a Japanese restaurant. Like many small Asian businesses, the wages were paid under the table and she was not included as a formal employee. In spite of the low pay, our frugality and belief that the situation was temporary allowed us to survive and even save small amounts of money for the future.

Adding to our financial difficulties was the increasing cost of housing. Every year, rent went up by 5% regardless of whether I was working or not. Bills come in on the same time every month, and there was always someone who needed to be paid. In between classes, I would go on job interviews looking for anything but without much success. I became dismayed by the negative responses I received and was even thrown out of one interview because of the way I looked. I would get a lot of "we will call you" types of answers, and tension for my family's survival heightened.

School fees have increased every year since I started school. When I first started California State University, Northridge, my tuition was approximately $1,500 a semester. In my last semester, it was more than $2,500. For students who are dependent on their parents, they might not know the significance of such an increase, but when you are on your own and you don't have any reliable source of income, it can be terrifying. We were forced to live solely on credit cards. The interest rates on my credit cards went from 10% to 29% over the course of two years. I looked for jobs on- and off-campus and applied for work study.

By December 2008, my wife and I were truly struggling. We were forced to apply for California food stamps. For those who are not familiar with the program, it is designed to help you pay for food in times of economic difficulty. The reason they are called food stamps is because one would actually use stamps to pay for food. Today, one is given a debit card, called an EBT card. This allows for greater privacy even though grocery clerks still know the method that you use to pay. The food stamps provided $250 a month to be allotted for food by the state of California. This was very helpful because my wife and I could then use the money we would have used on food to pay for other expenses, as well as save so that we would not have to continue to depend on food stamps.

The food stamp program didn't come without strings. Every month you are sent a QR7, which is a form with which you have to verify your income and eligibility for food stamps. If you do not fill out this form, then you lose your food stamps regardless of need or merit. One of the worst things about going onto food stamps is the stigma that you are hit with from other people. Even asking the question "Do you take food stamps?" at stores can cause embarrassment. The clerks and the other people in line look down at you. Their responses are not always intentional, but they reflect problematic American values of merit and work that are often ingrained and automatic. There is an idea that if you have food stamps you are a lazy freeloader who plans to abuse the welfare system. Also, most people believe that once you are on the system you will never get off of it. They fail to realize there are many people who need help, and once they get back on their feet they discontinue their use of the program.

No one should ever have to feel ashamed that they have food stamps. There is never a reason that your pride should come between you taking care of your family. California and other states need to have government assistance programs because families cannot always take care of the burden by themselves. The playing field is not always equal, and America is not based on a meritocracy. Without these programs, my wife and I would not have made it through the economic recession; I would not have been able to even graduate. The financial and emotional support that we have received has allowed us to stay on our feet and provided hope and opportunity. I plan to continue onto graduate school in the hope of gaining a better financial future for my family and to help me be an asset to my community. Like many others, regardless of what happens, we will continue to be resilient and move forward.

SECTION 3

Social and Community Support and Transformation

Gina Masequesmay

In Critical Race Theory work, the concept of cultural community asset is used to emphasize the positive traits of ethnic communities to adapt as opposed to the dominant view of racial communities as disorganized and pathological.[1] From this perspective, stories in which low-income, ethnic communities that pull resources together to provide their members with economic, social, and cultural support represent counternarratives. Instead of viewing racial communities as culturally or economically deficient and politically debilitated, the shift to agency emphasizes the ability for immigrant families to be resourceful in efforts to combat racist structural inequalities. In fact, oppositional behaviors and oppositional identity are seen as resistance to the racist mainstream society.[2] In this section, we focus on the ability of immigrant families to remain resilient through collective acts of resistance against oppressive conditions.

---

[1] Tara J. Yosso, *Critical Race Counterstories along the Chicana/Chicano Educational Pipeline* (New York: Routledge, 2006).

[2] Signithia Fordham and John U. Ogbu, "Black Students' School Success: Coping with the 'Burden of Acting White,'" *Urban Review* 18 (1986): 176–206.

Immigrant Community Cultural Assets

Shifting from the individual to acknowledging the significance of family and community in resilience work parallels immigrant studies that shift from human capital (knowledge, skills, and education), physical capital (money), and cultural capital (middle-class values and knowledge) to social capital. Social capital acknowledges the significance of social, economic, and cultural resources from ethnic/racial communities in adaptation. Specifically, social capital is the capacity to access resources from one's social network. For example, belonging to an ethnic community, immigrant coethnics are able to rely on each other for economic support, especially with loans for entrepreneurship, a feasible and reliable means for immigrant economic upward mobility.[3] Moreover, scholars have argued that the concentration of immigrant entrepreneurships in neighborhoods has created an ethnic enclave economy that provides an alternative mode of economic adaptation compared to the mainstream primary labor market.[4] An ethnic enclave economy serves as a concentration of businesses specifically targeting the ethnic, immigrant community's needs such as ethnic food, translation services, and health and legal needs in the ethnic language.

Other studies of immigrants emphasized how ethnic concentrations (ethnic enclave instead of ethnic enclave economy) have also provided other social and cultural support that immigrants often need. For example, immigrant ethnic churches and temples provide not only spiritual bonding but can become a hub for information distribution in terms of jobs, housing, and social services.[5] Moreover, ethnic immigrant networks provide members with a sense of belonging and ethnic pride that are often suppressed or marginalized in mainstream culture. In fact, resources within an ethnic network or social capital can offer a more positive adaptation for immigrant children than assimilation to the local culture and structure of poverty.[6,7] The concept of ethnic enclaves encompasses not only economic but also social and cultural support that provide for a segmented assimi-

---

[3] Ivan Light and Edna Bonacich, *Immigrant Entrepreneurs* (Los Angeles: University of California Press, 1988).

[4] Kenneth L. Wilson and Alejandro Portes, "Immigrant Enclaves: An Analysis of the Labor Market Experiences of Cubans in Miami," *American Journal of Sociology* 86 (1980): 295–319.

[5] Pyong Gap Min, "The Structure and Social Functions of Korean Immigrant Churches in the United States," *International Migration Review* 26, no. 4 (1992): 1370–1394.

[6] Alejandro Portes, "Children of Immigrants: Segmented Assimilation and Its Determinants," in *The Economic Sociology of Immigration: Essays on Networks, Ethnicity, and Entrepreneurship,* ed. A. Portes (New York: Russell Sage Foundation, 1995).

[7] Min Zhou, "Social Capital and the Adaptation of Second Generation: The Case of Vietnamese Youth in New Orleans," *International Migration Review* 28, no. 4 (1994):821–845.

lation that buffers immigrant children from assimilating into the underclass and allows them to hold onto their ethnic culture.

Whereas past immigrant studies frame the issues in terms of how well immigrants adapt to the mainstream society, these studies that focus on assets within the immigrant communities offer another perspective on how immigrants create more economic opportunities for themselves despite their impoverished surroundings and do not need to assimilate to mainstream culture. This system of financial and emotional support provided by the ethnic community helps immigrants build resilience that helps them face the daily challenges exacerbated in times of economic crisis.

Resilience as Resistance

In a 2001 article in *Urban Education,* Critical Race Theory scholars Daniel Solórzano and Dolores Delgado Bernal documented how student activists developed their social justice values from role models and mentors as they engaged in extracurricular activities.[8] Involvement in such activities raised and fortified students' social, cultural, and/or class consciousness, as well as their hope and desire to change oppressive social conditions. Through this work Solórzano and Delgado Bernal distinguished four types of behavior they deemed "oppositional" to the contexts in which students worked: reactionary behavior, self-defeating resistance, conformist resistance, and transformational resistance.

Reactionary behavior is manifested when students behave in opposition to mainstream standards but do so without a critique of their oppressive conditions or an interest in social justice. An example of reactionary behavior includes students who act out for the sake of being defiant and without a social consciousness. Unlike this first form of oppositional behavior, the three remaining can be seen as forms of resistance because people who engage in such action are either motivated by a social justice interest or are critical of the oppressive status quo.

The classic form of oppositional behavior is self-defeating resistance, which is when students have some critique of their oppressive social conditions but are not motivated by an interest in social justice to liberate them. Instead they engage in behaviors that are self-defeating, such as dropping out of school. Opposite of that is conformist resistance where youth are motivated by social equity and work

[8] Daniel Solórzano and Dolores Delgado Bernal, "Examining Transformational Resistance through a Critical race and LatCrit Theory Framework. Chicana and Chicano Student in an Urban Context," *Urban Education* 36, no. 2 (2001): 308–342.

within the system to improve themselves but without a critique of social oppression. The last type of oppositional behavior is transformational resistance where students critique oppression and work toward social justice. It is a form of resistance that is not for mere survival but for liberation.[9] In resisting the oppressive structure and in working toward self-efficacy and empowerment, students work toward individual and collective levels of social and political transformation. For Solórzano and Delgado Bernal, transformational resistance is the highest level of resistance or liberation when both normative ideology and structure are challenged. The stories of immigrants presented in this section constitute examples of types of resistance that highlight the ethnic community and social networks as sites of resilience building.

Immigrants' Stories of Resilience with the Support of Their Ethnic Communities

The stories in this section provide examples of individual, family, and community responses to The Great Recession with emphasis on the role of family, neighborhood, and religious and student networks as sites for surviving, resisting, and challenging the dominant system of inequalities.

In the stories by Carlos Jimenez and Anita Arce, we see a similar theme of family and religious networks as resources that help these individuals and their families through economic crises of unemployment and debt payment. In the case of Carlos, who became unemployed during The Great Recession, he was able to draw on family connections for spiritual guidance and rely on his newly found spiritual network for strength and faith in life. Having found resilient faith, he is able to cope with the uncertainties of unemployment. Similarly, Anita's journey consisted of help from family members, neighbors, and members of her Catholic church. Facing home foreclosure, bankruptcy, and scam artists who exacerbated her financial woes, she was able to obtain financial advice and services for free from a fellow church member to refinance her loans and save her house.

For Hyeyoung Kwon's interviewee, Jiwon, and language brokers like them, their human capital of bilingualism not only helped them individually but their families to cope with economic and acculturation stress. In some way, Jiwon's story is a typical working-class immigrant story, where the children's ability to learn a new language becomes a buttress for family survival. But, her story also chal-

[9] Tracie Robinson and Janie Ward, "'A Belief in Self Far Greater than Anyone's Disbelief': Cultivating Resistance among African American Female Adolescents," *Women & Therapy* 11, no. 3–4 (1991): 87–103.

lenges presumptions of dominant and normative child development in the Western society, where the work and productivity of children are understood to be hallmarks of the past. Language brokers perform complex tasks for their family and need to navigate confusing bureaucratic institutions while their parents maneuver through immigration settlement. Family responsibility and obligation often take a toll on these language brokers, but fortunately for Jiwon, she has a second home in her church. Through her Korean church network, Jiwon is able to find resources, guidance, and emotional support from her church "moms" and "brothers and sisters" to sustain her. Here, we see an example of how individual resilience and family resilience interact and are fed by communal resilience.

These three stories of resilience can be categorized as between conformist and transformative resistance with the last story having more critique of social oppression than the first two. The last two stories in this section are about transformative resistance at a community-based organization and a university campus. Through collective actions, both stories discuss the individual and collective levels of ideological and material transformation.

Wanda Pathomrit's story is an interweave of three stories about the Thai Community Development Center (Thai CDC) that fights for Thai immigrant rights, Wanda's involvement with this organization, and the struggles of Boon, a Thai worker who was helped by Thai CDC. In this story, Wanda documents her own social, cultural, and political consciousness development as a Thai immigrant and her reaffirmed commitment toward community empowerment via her work with Thai CDC. In Wanda's story of Boon, who was trafficked in this country to work as practically slave labor, she also accounts for how Thai CDC as a community resource center has not only aided Boon, but hundreds others like him to obtain social justice. Ironically, as Thai CDC is doing this empowerment work for the Thai community, its own program is at stake as the economic crisis has resulted in funding cuts. Yet, from the fifteen years of community empowerment work and the commitment of its staff, the reader is left optimistic to believe that Thai CDC will find a way to fund its projects to serve a marginalized community.

Furthest along the spectrum of transformational resistance, we find Jean-Paul deGuzman's story of enduring resilience from undocumented students at UCLA as they organize to obtain an affordable education via AB 540 and legal status via the DREAM Act. Jean-Paul accounts how a coalition of diverse students has created a new consciousness of interconnectedness that motivates students to fight for those less fortunate than themselves. Through teach-ins and protests, experiences and perspectives of undocumented students are humanized, and students learned of their own agency to make change. According to Jean-Paul, making the link between today's public education challenges and the larger historical issues provides students with tools to be intellectually and pragmatically resilient. Emboldened by their collective actions, students begin to question the current economic reality and to envision a new reality.

As the economic crisis strikes hard at education, demands for structural change seem far-fetched. As academic programs are being cut left and right, it does seem incredible that the DREAM Act discussion has not dropped from discourse thanks mainly to the courageous acts of these students. Indeed, this collectivization of ideas and actions by students has built a new infrastructure of activism that cannot be dismantled and will weather this economic storm. And, perhaps it is that idea to dream beyond the DREAM Act that will be resilient and transformative. If not materially then at least ideologically, these dreams will brew into future student and community movements.

Bibliography

Fordham, Signithia, and John U. Ogbu. "Black Students' School Success: Coping with the 'Burden of Acting White'." *Urban Review* 18 (1986): 176–206.

Light, Ivan, and Edna Bonacich. *Immigrant Entrepreneurs*. Los Angeles: University of California Press, 1988.

Min, Pyong Gap. "The Structure and Social Functions of Korean Immigrant Churches in the United States." *International Migration Review* 26, no. 4 (1992): 1370–1394.

Portes, Alejandro. "Children of Immigrants: Segmented Assimilation and Its Determinants." In *The Economic Sociology of Immigration: Essays on Networks, Ethnicity, and Entrepreneurship*, 248–280. Ed. Alejandro Portes. New York: Russell Sage Foundation. 1995.

Robinson, Tracie, and Janie Ward. "A Belief in Self Far Greater than Anyone's Disbelief': Cultivating Resistance among African American Female Adolescents." *Women & Therapy* 11, no. 3–4 (1991): 87–103.

Solórzano, Daniel, and Dolores Delgado Bernal. "Examining Transformational Resistance through a Critical race and LatCrit Theory Framework. Chicana and Chicano Student in an Urban Context." *Urban Education* 36, no. 2 (2001): 308–342.

Wilson, Kenneth L., and Alejandro Portes. "Immigrant Enclaves: An Analysis of the Labor Market Experiences of Cubans in Miami." *American Journal of Sociology* 86 (1980): 295–319.

Yosso, Tara J. *Critical Race Counterstories along the Chicana/Chicano Educational Pipeline*. New York: Routledge, 2006.

Zhou, Min. "Social Capital and the Adaptation of Second Generation: The Case of Vietnamese Youth in New Orleans." *International Migration Review* 28 (1994): 821–845.

13

Resiliency through Spiritual Means

Carlos Jiménez

I am a fifty-four-year-old husband and father of three who emigrated from Mexico in 1976. My first attempt at crossing the U.S.–Mexican border was unsuccessful because border patrol agents apprehended me while I was walking through a desolate area in San Isidro, California. Consequently, I spent two days in jail and was later deported back to Mexico. Although I was upset because I was caught, I did not become discouraged because two days after being deported, I attempted to cross once again. With the aid of a coyote (human smuggler), whom I paid $200, my second attempt proved successful. My journey took me through San Diego's mountains. Eventually, I walked across the border for about an hour and a half until I arrived—with others—at the apartment in which the coyote had designated for us to meet. From this location I boarded a van and was driven to Los Angeles.

My first two years in the United States were tough because I encountered numerous periods of unemployment. However, in 1978, my problem with sporadic employment ended when I was given a job at U.S.A. Petroleum as a part-time cashier. After only a week, I was given a full-time position, and three months later I was promoted to manager. I attribute my rapid mobility up the ranks to the manager I befriended and to my math skills. My manager liked me, and he soon realized that I was good at math—the result of being a former engineering student—so he did everything in his power to see that I was quickly promoted.

Eventually, I would remain an employee of U.S.A. Petroleum and later the Tesoro Corporation—which bought out the former—until 2009.

My thirty-one-year career came to an abrupt end during the fall of 2009 when I was laid off. It was hard to cope with the fact that I no longer had a job. Although I did not experience any symptoms of depression, I did begin to experience high levels of stress. Waking up in the morning became a daily ordeal for me because my economic future was now uncertain. I realized that my age and the country's economic turmoil were two factors that were going to contribute to my difficulty in finding employment. Consequently, this is exactly why I have filled out numerous applications, but employers have not responded. Furthermore, my first couple of months of being unemployed were difficult to adapt to because throughout the last thirty-one years there were periods of time where I worked two or even three jobs. Having nothing to do was another factor that was contributing to my stress. Nevertheless, as a result of losing my job, I was forced to make financial cut-backs, but fortunately I still have money for the basic necessities, such as the mortgage, groceries, and household bills. I have always emphasized the importance of saving money; now I am just glad that I listened to my own advice or else my unemployment would have been much more stressful. Eventually, spirituality would become my coping mechanism.

The ability to cope with my unemployment is attributed to a religious retreat that I participated in during the month of November 2009. This retreat took place in the hills adjacent to my native *pueblo* of Zacoalco de Torres, which is located in the state of Jalisco. During my time at the retreat, I lived in a cabin and spent my days fasting, praying, working, and meditating. Although all these aspects attributed to my spiritual growth, the time I endured in a hole was the most significant. An important aspect of the retreat requires participants to spend some time in a hole that is five feet deep and three feet in diameter. The amount of time that a participant can endure is entirely up to them. I spent a total of twenty-four hours in the hole; in which I fasted—including water—and prayed the entire time. The ordeal is similar to what monks used to participate in during past centuries. I must admit that the hole was very uncomfortable because it was not large enough to stand in and I only had the option of sitting or kneeling on a dirt floor. However, I was able to overcome this test because I was offering my penance to God. Overall, the retreat helped me to find meaning in everything. I found a spiritual awakening and, as a result, peace as well. When I returned home, I realized that I was no longer worried about my job or money. Somehow, I knew things were going to work out.

My spiritual awakening influenced me to begin reading more spiritual literature. Although reading has always contributed to my growth as a person, the books that I used to spend most of my time reading pertained to business, communication, investments, human behavior, and secular self-help books—never spiritual. Since my return from the retreat, spiritual literature has taken a priority in my life. Interestingly enough, I was able to make connections between the spiritual books and some of the books I used to read. I discovered that many of the quotes that I found in the secular literature were references from the Bible. I guess that is why they call it, "The Good Book." Nonetheless, my new-found interest in spiritual literature will hopefully help me build a closer and stronger relationship with God. This is important because it is through God's grace that I have been able to cope with my problem.

When I returned from the retreat I found myself having a keen interest in participating in my wife's prayer group. My wife (Maria Jiménez) has been a devout Catholic and spiritual healer for many years. Throughout the years, she has devoted much of her time to providing emotional and spiritual help for people in need. These people are often very sick or are experiencing some other type of life crisis. Consequently, participating in this group has also been very beneficial to me because it is not only a support group for strangers, but also for those within the inner circle. We regularly pray for one another and articulate our problems with one another. Therefore, the group has provided spiritual healing and therapeutic counseling. Furthermore, the people that we pray for have given me the strength and courage I need to overcome my own dilemma—being unemployed.

Although my entire family has been supportive, I think that I owe a great deal of appreciation to my wife, Maria, and my nephew, Alan Castro. If it were not for my wife, I doubt that I would have ever attended the retreat that proved so beneficial to my well-being. She was the one who constantly insisted that I attend the retreat; she obviously had a good reason for doing so. Moreover, my nephew—who was planning on becoming a priest until not too long ago—is the other reason why I have been able to cope with my unemployment problem. Several years ago, my father gave him a piece of land that is now used to facilitate the retreats. I thank my nephew for creating these retreats that have not only been helpful to me, but for hundreds of people as well. Priests from Mexico and the United States, along with non-clerical people, have flocked to Alan's retreats to seek spiritual guidance and growth. The retreat I attended in November 2009 was so beneficial to me that I am going to return to Mexico again to attend another one. We all need help during times of crisis; fortunately, I was blessed with two people who were crucial to my spiritual growth. They were my links to a spiritual community that supported and lifted me from the darkness of unemployment with resilient faith to cope with life's adversities.

14

The Support in My Life/Navigating the Financial Maze

Anita Arce

My name is Anita Arce, and I am forty-six years old. Twenty years ago, I came to the United States from El Salvador with my two daughters, and I identify myself as Latin American. Like many others, I was forced to leave my country for political reasons because my ex-husband was a very active political leader against the government. His involvement became so dangerous that we had to leave the country, leaving everything behind. Since then, life has not been easy for us.

We crossed the border through the airport, pretending to be gardeners in a work truck. Our journey took us three weeks before we finally arrived in Los Angeles. Ten months after we arrived in the United States, my husband and I separated, and thus, I was left alone in a new country with two daughters, who were four and seven years old at that time. I had never worked a day in my life and did not even have the advantage of speaking English. There were not many opportunities for a woman in my circumstances. The only option left for me was to work hard to receive a formal education if I wanted to succeed. Working a full-time job and going to school was not easy, but I have been fortunate to have my children, who have always provided me with emotional support.

My sister was a very important source of support for me in the years following my divorce. She and I have always been very close, and when I decided to come to the United States, she agreed to come with me. She also had a child, a little boy who was ten months younger than my youngest daughter. Once in the United States, we found that we had to rely on each other a lot if we were going to not only survive but also help our own children succeed. Her help did not only stop at financial support but came in a number of other ways. Living together, we were able to help each other out in everyday expenses such as paying groceries, rent, and other maintenance bills. She also made it possible for me to attend night school by taking care of my daughters at night while I was in class. Had it not been for her, I would not be in the process of getting my credentials today. She was not the only one to provide support, though.

The apartment complex where I used to live was small but full of people that were able to help one another. When I began to work, my youngest daughter was not old enough to go to school yet. My upstairs neighbor, who had a son about the same age as my daughter, offered to take care of her for me until either my sister or I got home. Although I did pay her, this was not very much since we were friends, and I would take care of her son whenever she had to work. Besides the neighbor who provided childcare, there were other people who helped me to acculturate into the new world that this country was for me. There was a lady that took me to the elementary school nearby and translated for me so I could enroll my daughters at school. She also helped me fill out any paperwork that was required. Another woman from the apartment complex helped me find a job once I had separated from my husband. Had it not been for her it may have been much more difficult for me to find a job since I knew very few people outside of the complex. Many of these people were immigrants from Armenia, and others were from several Central American countries. They had gone through similar experiences upon their arrival to the United States and were, therefore, able to understand and sympathize with what I was going through as a single mother.

Since then, I have remarried and have a four-year-old son from my second marriage. My sister moved to another state with her family about fourteen years ago due to the lack of available jobs in California, but we are still very close and try to help each other whenever we can. For a long period of time, my financial situation was good. It may not have been perfect, but it was good enough that we had the most important things. My husband used to work in construction, and he had enough work to keep us financially stable.

Unfortunately, the recent economic crash hit the housing market first. His work opportunities started to appear less and less every day while the cost of construction materials started to rise. Other factors also affected our financial situation such as tuition fee hikes and skyrocketing mortgage payments. At the same time, we had a newborn for whom to provide.

It seemed like my economic problems were getting worse and worse day-by-day, along with my stress. We got to the point of having to stop making our house payments and of me considering leaving school and getting an extra job. Providing a house for my daughters and getting my teaching credentials had been my main goals since I had arrived. Thus, I did not know which goal I should give up first. As a single mother, I had worked very hard in order to save the money that I would need for the mortgage entrance or down payment. While we were struggling financially, my husband and my daughters always told me to stay in school. They believed that it was much easier to start over with a house than with my education. Morally supported by my family, I continued with school but had to take on school loans to help cover my fees as well as my costs of living. My husband was unable to continue with his construction work and got a different job. During the day, he took a part-time job as a valet and at night he worked as a security guard for a filming company; both jobs that he continues till today. Even with the new arrangement, we were unable to keep up with the mortgage payments and so I began to try to negotiate with the banks. Unfortunately, they would not accept partial payments, and I was forced to look for other sources to help me. I hired a company to represent me and worked with the banks in order to see if that would work better, but all they did was take my money. As a result, my house was scheduled for sale on May 18, 2009.

I was frustrated and desperate and found that the only option I could see was to file for bankruptcy. I was led to this decision by a group, which I had found from a flyer. This group had passed flyers throughout the neighborhood because there were a number of houses that had foreclosed in our community. When I hired this group and we had gone over all the options that were available to me, they told me that filing for Chapter 13 was my best and only option. This option would allow me to keep my house and begin making payments again as long as a judge approved the bankruptcy claim. Yet, this did not turn out to be the simple solution I was told it would be. In the process of filing Chapter 13, all my credit card debts, two mortgages, and all the lawyer and court fees were put together. This ended up being worse because the payments I had to make were so high that in only five months I was right back to where I had started. I decided to stop the Chapter 13 process and look around for other avenues of help.

Between my job, school, and taking care of my son, there never seems to be enough time to socialize. Fortunately, Sunday mass allows me to socialize with other church members, as I am a regular member of my Catholic church and an assistant to the Sunday service. Socialization occurs after mass when church members sell food in order to raise money for the poor. Usually at the end of the service, a member of the church goes up to the podium and announces the events in the upcoming weeks and the services that the church will be providing. One day, the announcer informed us that the church was going to be holding a workshop for people who were interested in buying a house. The workshop was mainly designed to teach the buyer how to deal with all of the paperwork involved and how to lower the price and interest rate. Although the workshop did not seem to offer anything to someone in my position, I decided to make an appointment with the consultant anyway.

When I went to meet the consultant in the church's breakfast room, I explained to him my problem, and he told me that although he could not help me himself, he did know of someone who could. This person, he said, worked in loan modifications and could possibly help me. He gave me the man's contact information and suggested I call. The man he told me to contact was a loan consultant who also happened to be a licensed realtor. I spoke with this loan consultant and he said he would gladly help me. I was a bit wary about this person at first, because I believed that this person could very well be like all of the other people whom I had hired and had done nothing but take my money and complicate matters more. Fortunately, this man was different. When I met with him, he told me that a brother from church had asked him to help me and, therefore, he was going to do it at no charge to me. He believed that my case was not all that difficult to resolve and that within a month we would have an answer from the bank. He was right; about one month later the bank gave me a six-month payment plan. During these six months, I had to give the bank all of the paperwork that they required and make all the payments they had set on time. At the end of those six months, they granted me the loan modification and added all of the back payments I owed them as part of the total mortgage loan. This was done, not because they wanted to help me, but because they were afraid they were not going to get any of the money I owed. In the end, the loan consultant helped me more than any of the lawyers and other services I had hired. My church is a great source of information; people can benefit even if they are not members of the church because they distribute flyers with all the information for the public. It is also a good way to get to know people and help each other out—much like the person who helped me get in contact with the consultant that helped me.

I have no words to explain how happy I am now, having been able to overcome the obstacles that I have faced, mainly the potential loss of my home during this recent economic crisis. I am very grateful for all the people that have aided me in my times of need; beginning with those I met as a new immigrant in this country and ending with those I have met recently through church. It is my hope that one day I will be able to provide someone with the same type of support that all of the people in my life have given me.

15

From Human Capital to Community Resource: Language Brokering Work as Survival and Strength

Hyeyoung Kwon

I was fourteen years old when I boarded an airplane to America. I remember I was so excited that I couldn't sleep a wink for the entire thirteen-hour flight. My head swam with thoughts about all the glitz and glamour of Hollywood that I had seen on television while growing up. Upon arrival, however, reality hit hard for my parents. They had to find jobs and look for an apartment. Despite their economic struggles, they tried to hide their financial problems from me so I could devote my time and energy to school. But as time passed, I found myself helping my parents establish a permanent settlement in Los Angeles. My dad relied on my broken English when signing the rental contract with our landlord. My mother asked me to help complete her job applications. My parents could no longer hide their financial troubles from me when I had to look over their credit card and bank statements. It was because of this personal experience that I wanted to learn more about the hardships of language brokers from a working-class background. What is it like for language brokers to grow up in a low-income neighborhood during an economic recession? What do they learn from this experience? How do they cope with the overwhelming sense of responsibility once they learn of their families' personal woes through translation activities?

To answer this question, I ventured into Koreatown, the place where I grew up. The majority of Koreatown residents suffer from poverty and language barriers. Behind the cosmopolitan image of Los Angeles Koreatown, with its new luxurious condos and nightclubs, there are the faces of poor immigrants. They sell and serve ethnic food at the Korean supermarkets and restaurants—the top two employers in the enclave. They work long hours but still fail to bring home enough income for their families. In 2003, when the Korean Immigrant Workers Advocates (KIWA) released their report on Koreatown, the Koreatown families' median household income was $20,000 compared to the Los Angeles County average of $42,000. The recession hit them hard. They only made 83% of the income they earned during the 1990s.

This story focuses on Jiwon[10], a Koreatown resident and resilient language broker who immigrated to the United States when she was eight. Using snowball sampling, I've talked to twenty-five language brokers from Koreatown. Out of all the interviews, I find her story most compelling because, unlike many language brokers who reported that their supposedly protected stage of life was interrupted by their translation work, Jiwon displayed a great sense of pride and optimism. I learned a great deal about how she navigates societal constraints through her translation works that she performed on her father's behalf. To remain resilient, Jiwon redefined the meaning of family and home in this process.

Like many other immigrant teenagers, translation activities are ordinary and everyday experiences for Jiwon. She checks phone messages, sorts out mail, writes checks to pay bills, and calls or visits government bureaus (e.g., DMV, court, immigration and unemployment office) for her dad. These ordinary experiences, however, revealed her dad's "secret" last year. Jiwon saw her dad's credit card debts building up and his bank account getting over-drafted. Financial problems eventually broke her parents apart. Her mom, who maneuvered through different jobs ranging from supermarket cashier to restaurant waitress, filed for a divorce this year and left the house with Jiwon's older brother. Later, Jiwon learned that her mom gave up paying for the credit card debts that her dad accumulated over a few months and chose divorce as a way out. Jiwon vividly remembered how sad she was when her mother gave up on her own family. "Back then, I didn't quite understand why my mom chose the easy way out . . . the worst part of translating for my dad was letting him know that he got the divorce papers. I was home that day, when he opened the door and brought in that big yellow envelope. I took a look at it and told him, 'Dad, they are divorce papers' in Korean." Jiwon said it with a wry smile.

[10] I used a pseudonym in this story to protect the identity of the interviewee.

The problem worsened. One day, when Jiwon came home from school, she found her dad in the living room, waiting for Jiwon with a pile of documents. That day, when she called the unemployment agency on behalf of her dad, she learned that he was laid off from his previous job and had not found another one. Unlike her mom, who had better opportunities in feminized service-oriented jobs in the ethnic enclave, finding a job was always a challenge for her dad. Both her mom and dad had limited resources, education, and English proficiency, but Jiwon observed that, regardless of their background, there were simply not many jobs available for Korean immigrant men. Jiwon's dad first worked for his brother, the owner of a wholesale apparel business in downtown Los Angeles, who sponsored her family to come to the United States. When his brother's business got scaled down due to the recent economic recession, Jiwon's dad had to find a job elsewhere.

Jiwon had no idea that her dad was laid off for a while since he still left the house in the morning and came home at night. "My dad is a typical Korean man who doesn't like to share his feelings" she said, "plus, I am sure he had so much pride in being a breadwinner." Everything started making sense for Jiwon. She now understood why her dad did not have any money in the bank account, accumulated credit card debts, and could not stop her mom from leaving.

Despite some of the worried and wry statements she made, Jiwon took enormous pride in her language brokering work. When she finished the translation works, she saw the results immediately: late fees on her dad's credit card had gone down and he began receiving unemployment benefits. More importantly, she was proud of what her bilingual skills can do for her family. But, she also acknowledged that it was extremely difficult for her to understand the jargon that appeared in the government documents. "Why don't they make it simpler? It feels as if they don't want the applicants to understand the whole process. Not everyone is educated in the United States, even if they are adults." Behind her complaint, there was a lingering sense of anger about the unjust system that denies the resources and access to poor monolingual immigrants. However, she took out the dictionary and learned the nitty-gritty of California labor law before speaking to a representative at the unemployment office.

Jiwon, like many other language brokers I interviewed, described herself as a "fighter" in their family. It took initiative and assertiveness for teenagers like Jiwon to deal with the complexity of bureaucracy and "scary" and "grumpy" government personnel. Jiwon recalled some credit card agency representatives who refused to talk to a "child," even though they did not have a Korean translator available for her dad. She did not back down. She changed her voice to sound like an adult. When one representative did not want to reduce late fees on her dad's credit card debt, she even asked to speak with the supervisor. "I have to learn how to talk to them," she said with the deep conviction in her voice, "because my family's economic survival sometimes depends on me." There was calmness and charisma in her voice.

Language brokers' work from low-income families brings its own special problems. Finding out "too much" about their parents' financial and family problems brings emotional distress and anxiety. Jiwon, who recently got accepted into the University of California, Irvine, had mixed feelings about this good news initially. She knew that her dad would be extremely happy if he found out, but she also recognized that her dad did not have enough money to send her to college. She also worried about leaving her dad who always relied on her for translation support.

After holding onto the acceptance letter for a few days, Jiwon decided to take it to her pastor at church. Her pastor gave her a warm hug and asked her not to worry about money. He helped her apply for financial aid and church-sponsored scholarships. "Honestly, church is like my second home. I love my dad, but sometimes I want to get away from debtors and my dad who sighs all the time," she imitated her dad sighing.

Escaping anxiety at her own home, Jiwon has created another home at her church, and this second home provided her with social, financial, and emotional support. She obtained crucial information on how to apply for financial aid and was able to reduce her fatigue and stress by sharing her fear and hope. Her mom is not home, but there are a lot of "moms" cooking dinner for her at church. Her brother is no longer around, but there were many "brothers and sisters" who listened and guided her career plan.

Feeling grateful for all the help that she received from her church members, Jiwon now returns the favor by sharing her translation and bilingual skills with her church members. In this process she has turned her human capital into a community resource. Many adults at church now come to her with letters that they have received from the government. Jiwon proudly said that she recently helped a grandmother file for a citizenship application. Developing many trustful relationships with her church members—who are widely connected to resources—Jiwon has cultivated social capital in the form of a network that can be converted into resources. Her social capital even impacts her family's socioeconomic status as Jiwon now earns money as a tutor to a "younger sister" at church.

"I sometimes envy those people who have everything. Some people have parents who do everything for their children. But, if you don't have that kind of parents, you find ones by yourself. I also learned something that they would never know. I am tactical and I learned how to negotiate with those people in the system. I am sure these skills will help me down the line." Jiwon was very aware of the painful social inequalities, but she was not a passive victim. She actively contributed her bilingual skills for family survival, and now she has used her bilingual skills to help other immigrants in her community who are faced with language barriers. Jiwon's church has become her safe place and a second home where she has formed loving and trustful relationships with other church members. Moreover, the members of this new home appreciate Jiwon's accumulated and acquired language brokering skills. Her skills are no longer solely utilized as a family resource. Rather, these skills have become shared resources that make a significant difference in the community.

In television shows like *Leave It to Beaver* and *The Brady Bunch,* childhood seems so carefree. The family lives in a big suburban house with a white picket fence and a swimming pool. They have the loving soccer mom and the father who barbecues in the backyard every Sunday. Nowhere in these scenes do children console their parents and fight for their families' economic survival. Yet, Jiwon's compelling counter-story challenges us to re-evaluate these images that marginalize the life experiences of so many immigrant language brokers and problem solvers from low-income backgrounds.

16

Working Together for a Better World: Community Development and Social Work

Wanda Pathomrit

The federal government is proposing massive cuts of $61 billion in the current fiscal year budget, which means that Californians are potentially faced with a loss of $571 million to support social welfare, economic development, public safety, affordable housing, and many other programs that are essential lifelines during hard economic times. The budget cuts are negatively impacting everyone's ability to survive—especially non-profit organizations that provide social welfare programs. Nevertheless, I chose a career path in the non-profit sector because I believe social workers and non-profit community-based organizations (CBOs) are the frontline community soldiers fighting injustice and poverty to increase the quality of life for vulnerable low-income families and unprotected immigrant populations. Not surprisingly, my passion for social work grew from my roots of growing up in an immigrant family.

My parents immigrated in the 1980s as part of the third wave of low-skilled workers, street merchants, and vendors who migrated to the United States and became vulnerable undocumented laborers. I grew up directly exposed to the issues of Thai immigrants facing exploitation, poverty, and cultural language barriers. In my early childhood, the restaurants were my second home, where my mother worked fourteen hours a day with no breaks. I often witnessed my mother being yelled at by her boss, "Ahi sat tam ngaan hai rew rew" or "You animal work faster!" My mother strained a smile through her hardship and kept working in order to save enough money for my entire family to reunite in the United States. My family's struggles resemble those of many other Thai immigrant families trying to attain the American dream of one day owning a family restaurant or business. For me, however, my family's struggles have also inspired me to work for the non-profit organization, Thai Community Development Center (Thai CDC). It is in Thai CDC's mission "to advance the social and economic well-being of low and moderate income Thais and other ethnic communities in the greater Los Angeles area through a comprehensive community development strategy including human rights advocacy, affordable housing, access to healthcare, promotion of small businesses, neighborhood empowerment, and social enterprises" that I see values enacted.

At Thai CDC, I have an invaluable opportunity to work with the most vulnerable people in the Thai community and to serve Thai CDC's goal of economic and social sustainability. The director of Thai CDC, Chancee Martorell, has placed me alongside a team of passionate staff and volunteers to learn how to become an advocate for human trafficking victims and their family members to overcome the stress of economic and cultural dislocation and displacement. The organization provides an immediate response team that arranges shelter, food, clothing, medical care, and legal counsel for the victims. Most importantly, we help survivors overcome their trauma, develop their survival and self-sufficiency skills, and prepare them to seek redress and restitution through various legal channels. As an advocate, I have an array of responsibilities aiding victims to overcome the language and cultural barriers by translating and documenting their stories for attorneys to help the victims file for T-visas that would grant them legal status and safety from retaliation. The T-visa allows victims of human trafficking and immediate family members to remain and work temporarily in the United States if they agree to assist law enforcement in testifying against the perpetrators. In addition, we provide comprehensive case management services, coordinating activities such as public transportation field trips and accompanying victims' families to enroll their children into public schools.

One of the most impactful works I have done at Thai CDC is becoming an advocate for Thai human trafficking survivors who were trafficked by Global Horizons, a labor contractor company. Thai CDC currently advocates for 263 victims who have been trafficked to the United States through the H-2A Visa Guest worker's program. Global Horizons trafficked workers through the recruitment company AACO. The recruiters made promises of high wages and a work contract to come to America as guest workers. However, the recruitment company required the workers to pay exorbitant recruitment fees, where recruitment agents arranged high interest loans with private third parties and had workers put up their ancestral land as collateral. Also, farm workers were not given a chance to read their employment agreements. Once the workers arrived in the United States, they were transported nationwide, including to Florida, Oregon, Washington, Utah, Hawaii, and Georgia. At different destinations their passports were confiscated, and they were threatened to be deported if they complained or did not work hard. For various months, workers lived in America without pay. Many of the farm workers incurred enormous amount of debts to come to America and feared they would not be able to pay back their debts. They lived in overcrowded and dangerous, uninhabitable environments such as sleeping in dirty, old, and abandoned houses with no heat or hot water and crates without windows or lights. Oftentimes, workers starved for food and would try to sneak into the forest or nearby farmlands to pick vegetables because there was insufficient amount of food given to the workers by the company. The workers were also threatened not to talk to outsiders. They only had each other to survive.

As an advocate, I have been very fortunate to work with Boon, one of the human trafficking victims. In Boon's case, the recruiter made false promises claiming, "If you come to work in the U.S. for three years, you will earn thousands of dollars a month to send back to your homeland in Lampang Province. You can never make that much money to support your family if you continue to work in Thailand." Thinking about his family, Boon sacrificed his life savings and put up his ancestral land for collateral to borrow a 300,000 Baht loan from the bank to pay for the recruitment fees. In actuality, when he came to the United States, his visa expired in less than a month and the immigration authorities deported him. He was sent back home with nothing but disappointment of unfulfilled promises. The recruiters forced him to pay an extra fee of 100,000 Baht in order to go back to the United States. Boon was angry and felt betrayed, but now he was enslaved by the debt he had incurred from the recruiter. He had no choice but to pay the fees. The recruiter sent Boon back to the U.S. where he worked in farms in Mississippi, Maryland, Georgia, and Hawaii. His employer confiscated his passport and isolated him and other Thai workers from outsiders. They were guarded by people posing to be immigration authorities and constantly were threatened to be deported if they failed to obey the rules. Boon eventually escaped in 2004 and came to Los Angeles. This was where he was able to get in contact with Thai CDC. He has been separated from his family for seven years and is still awaiting justice.

Thai CDC had reported Boon's case to the U.S. Department of Justice, the U.S. Department of Homeland Security, Immigration and Customs Enforcement, U.S. Equal Employment Opportunity Commission (EEOC), and the Royal Thai Consulate General of Los Angeles. Thai CDC has helped him file charges of employment discrimination and civil rights violations against Global Horizons. After five years of investigation, the EEOC held a press conference on April 20, 2011, announcing that they have filed a lawsuit against Global Horizons, the labor broker, and eight farms on behalf of Thai farm workers trafficked to Hawaii and Washington. Despite the federal government's slow response to assist the farm workers, Thai CDC has been collaborating with CAST (Coalition Abolishing Slavery and Trafficking) and various public and private legal firms to provide legal assistance in filing for T-visa applications for the farm workers.

In the five years since his escape, Boon has been working in Thai restaurants. His work includes washing dishes, cooking with heavy woks, taking out trash, and other various manual tasks. He skips meals and holds out on buying anything unnecessary so that he can make enough money to send back home to help pay debts. Currently, he has been diagnosed with cancer and his right arm is disabled from heavy work. He has been unemployed for ten months. He calls home occasionally in tears, realizing that he's not able to make any income to support the family. He expressed, "I was always taught to be the pillar of the family. My right arm and leg cannot work to pay back the debt. My wife has to do all the work of taking care of the family and my parents in Thailand. Sometimes I feel hopeless." Despite the challenges he encounters, as a Buddhist man, he accepts his fate and tries to always smile. He doesn't like to think about the past. I sit across from him interpreting for the attorney who is recording his statements. As he discloses his story, however, it becomes very hard for me to interpret the silent moments, when he looks at me at a loss for words to recount repressed memories hidden in the past. I use the language I learned from home to help give voice to his story so he can file for a T-visa in order to reunite with his family and attain justice. He misses his family dearly, and he discloses that "I've haven't seen my mother, wife and son forever. If I got to see my family right now, I would want to tell my son that I love him although I was never there to raise him."

Through Thai CDC initiatives, a third of the victims have filed for T-visas to the immigration authorities. Boon has now been granted a T-visa that allows him to file for social benefits. This would qualify him for medical benefits to obtain treatment and surgery for his cancer. He is truly a survivor and still continues to fight for justice by sharing his story with the world through Thai CDC's awareness campaign program, the Slavery Eradication and Rights Initiatives (The SERI Project). Boon will be featured in a documentary directed by Curtis McElhinney. Al Jazeera and other major news sources have interviewed him. Because there are pending trials against his traffickers, Boon still has to keep his identity a secret. In the interviews with the media, Boon never reveals his face to the camera. Boon feels very fortunate to be able to share his story and never hesitates to speak out when he gets the chance.

Sadly, however, all of the program benefits Boon has been receiving from Thai CDC could be completely eliminated due to the ending of the Anti-Human Trafficking Per Capita Contract Program. This program is administered by USCCB (United States Conference of Catholic Bishops), which receives its funding from the Federal Department of Health and Human Services. They allocate more than $100,000 in support of our social services. The funding will officially end on October 2011 and will not be renewed due to massive federal budget cuts. Thai CDC has only months to rapidly mobilize and find alternative funding sources. The consequences can be extremely detrimental to our ability to aid the ongoing Thai farm workers' cases. It is the largest human trafficking case in U.S. history. Currently, Thai CDC case managers work with numerous trafficked victims from all across the United States, serving 112 victims within California; 68 victims throughout Florida, Oregon, Washington, Utah, and Georgia; and 69 victims in Hawaii. We are alerting the media to help urge Congress to take immediate action towards the re-authorization of the TVPA (Trafficking Victim's Protection Act) in 2011 in order to continue the services for victims.

Boon's story reflects a struggle prevalent in America today against labor exploitation and modern day slavery. For some, America is not the land of dreams Boon had imagined. Human trafficking victims are deceived, abused, exploited, and isolated. Exacerbating this are cultural and language barriers that make it daunting to find justice for this very vulnerable and unprotected population. However, working with Boon made me realize how non-profit CBOs like Thai CDC truly serve as the lifeline and the bridge to overcome those barriers so that survivors can reclaim their lives and sustain social and economic well-being. In an interview Boon shared, "Without Thai CDC I could have been completely paralyzed or dead already. It is the voice that echoes my needs. I could not imagine my life without this organization."

As a Thai immigrant social worker, the work that I do at Thai CDC to empower my ethnic community is very meaningful to me at many levels. I see the value of Thai CDC in building resilience for the Thai American community. As I meet and develop relations with the workers and clients at Thai CDC, I begin to understand that Thai CDC is not just a non-profit organization that provides social and legal services for the Thai community; it is a reflection and manifestation of the resilience of my community to overcome obstacles and to obtain social justice.

17

Economic Realities and Student Dreams in the City of Angels

Jean-Paul R. deGuzman

The current economic meltdown has caused havoc across all public universities, particularly those in California. Although government-sanctioned assaults on public education are nothing new in the Golden State—a process largely catalyzed by the passage of the anti-taxation Proposition 13—the recent global collapse of financial markets has had a profound effect on the lives of students of color and working-class students.[11] This brief essay illustrates student activism at the University of California, Los Angeles, focusing on undocumented student activism and campus organizing in the midst of draconian budget cutbacks. We are living in difficult times that have amplified obstacles facing students in public schools. However, through collective action on campus and a commitment to critiquing the political and economic status quo in thought and deed, students have met the challenges of today's financial hardships with enduring resilience.

[11] Proposition 13 was a California ballot initiative spearheaded by insurgent anti-taxation activists committed to rolling back the perceived power of the state government. Passed by the electorate in 1978, it capped property taxes, essentially de-funding much of the state's public infrastructure.

To briefly explain my investment in these issues, I would like to rewind to 2008 when I was a first year student in UCLA's Ph.D. program in American history, and the nation was beginning to feel the initial pangs of the economic crisis. Although I had a background in activism and organizing from my undergraduate and graduate work in Asian American studies, I sought to broaden my understanding of community empowerment through the specific lens of labor organizing. Although institutionalized exclusions structured around race and gender characterize the vast majority of the history of the American labor movement, changes in immigration law in the 1960s and the restructuring of the U.S. economy in the 1970s have made it impractical for labor organizing to not address the issues of immigrant workers. Likewise, collective organizing has become an even more significant dimension of resiliency in immigrant communities to fight against economic, social, and political inequality. Even though the relationship between immigrant workers and the hierarchies of organized labor still remains contentious in some sectors, the mobilization of working peoples of all stripes has formed the architecture for a larger movement for social and economic justice, particularly in urban landscapes such as New York and Los Angeles.

With that knowledge in mind, I diverged from my graduate courses in historiography and took several service learning courses in Labor and Workplace Studies in addition to a seminar on the history of American labor in the twentieth century. Specifically I took a course that explored the intersections between labor, immigration, race, and higher education. As the new labor history has shown, progressive, working-class movements are not solely restricted to the workplace. Those movements also take place in the community and classroom and involve people of all ages.

Indeed, as my class outlined, students, often from immigrant and working-class backgrounds, have come to play a major role in injecting new energy, enthusiasm, and motivation into those movements. The students, predecessor to my seminar, produced the groundbreaking 2008 anthology *Underground Undergrads,* a collection of personal narratives and essays that explores the lives of undocumented students—youth who did not come to the United States on their own volition and are trapped in a state of legal limbo. My class continued that spirit, working with the UCLA Labor Center and our campus undocumented student organization IDEAS (Improving Dreams, Education, Access, and Success), to bring together scholars, activists, community members, cultural workers, and policy advocates for a day-long teach-in on two instrumental pieces of legislation critical for the empowerment of undocumented students. The first is California's Assembly Bill 540, which allows undocumented youth who have completed at least three years in a California high school and have been accepted to a college in California to pay in-state fees. The second is the proposed Federal Development, Relief, and Education for Alien Minors Act, better known as the DREAM Act which, if passed, would provide a conditional pathway to applying for citizenship for undocumented youth who graduated from high school, are of good moral character, and are completing their college education or serving in the armed forces (a dimension that has garnered astute criticism for the further militarization of immigrant communities). The teach-in involved a plenary session of leaders of the undocumented student movement as well as a range of student-initiated workshops on navigating the higher educational system, finding resources and support for undocumented youths, as well as planning strategies to advocate for the passage of the DREAM Act. Students from UCLA, the CSUs, community colleges, and even some high schools attended the teach-in, along with folks from local worker centers and labor unions who have made the struggle of undocumented youth a priority for their respective organizations.

My experiences with this and other labor and workplace studies courses exposed me to the urgency of reforming immigration law to empower countless undocumented students who, through the exigencies of a profoundly flawed immigration system and neoliberal political economy, have been relegated to the margins of society. Our teach-in was truly a collaboration of students and other activists both within and beyond UCLA and illustrated how weaving diverse strands of knowledge and talents could transform hope for a better future for immigrants into tangible action and resiliency. As a service learning class we continued to learn about the contours of agency—the quality and capability of making decisions in circumstances beyond our immediate control and working towards political and ideological change to alter the social structures around us. We learned of our own agency, but also how collaborative action can help bring out the agency in others. Indeed, it was our hope that our attendees would spread the knowledge, stories, experiences, and strategies we imparted even further to help fortify this immigrant rights movement and spark a spirit of resiliency in a time of otherwise dim prospects.

Flashing forward to the 2009–2010 academic year, students across the nation, but particularly in public schools in California, took to the streets to protest cuts to education budgets. The case of California was particularly alarming as the Regents of the University of California raised fees by some 30%, with the first hike to take place immediately. The UCLA campus erupted in protest as resources across campus, including a number of tutorial services, were either scaled back or eradicated wholesale. Progressive campus organizations mobilized students to walk out of their classes and join the spirited protests at Covel Commons, the location of the Fall 2009 UC Regents meeting as well as a once robust tutoring lab. These cuts affected all students, but the economic recession especially impacted the rhythm of daily life for students of color, first-generation students, immigrant students, and working-class students. As the late, great DREAM Activist Tam

Tran pointed out in her important film *Lost and Found,* undocumented students—generally shut out from financial aid opportunities—must work multiple jobs to the point of taking leaves of absence from coursework, to make ends meet. The economic crunch exacerbated an already precarious situation.

Indeed, the protest movements that took place in November 2009 and March 2010 at UCLA demonstrated the impact of the budget cuts on undocumented students. Amidst the panoply of protest signs—"Free the UC," "Stop the abuse," "Chop from the top," "education is a right," "End poverty @ UC," and "Spirit [UC President] Yudof AWAYYYY!"—one of the more grim reminders of the immediate impact of the challenge to inclusive and equitable public education was a black cardboard tombstone bearing the simple, yet sobering, words, "The 1st to Go: AB-540 Students."

Despite these seemingly insurmountable challenges, student activism has not withered at UCLA. Indeed, following the protests in November another series of actions took place on March 4, 2010. Student activism and resiliency go hand in hand. As I alluded to earlier, an important part of the protest actions were walkouts—a concerted effort to leave the classroom to demonstrate that students, from first year undergraduates to doctoral candidates, will not stand for the decimation of public education, drawing on the legacies of other student-of-color movements such as the historic East Los Angeles Blowouts and the establishment of Ethnic Studies programs at UCLA, San Fernando Valley State College, and Long Beach State College (now, CSU Northridge and Long Beach, respectively) in the 1960s and 1970s as well as the protests against the assault on affirmative action in the 1990s.

Of course, not all students felt compelled to join in the recent protests. There were students who remained in the classrooms. There was faculty who continued to lecture. There were also students who used the walkouts as an opportunity to ditch class. However, there were also countless students who stood up for their education and joined the protests to educate themselves and others about the severity of the attacks on colleges and universities. The courageous organizers for the protests embodied dedication to public education and hopefully empowered other students—immigrant or otherwise—to make serious decisions about how they would support their schools and fellow students. Beyond these living examples, student groups initiated teach-ins to keep the urgency of defending public education on the radar of every student and expose the increasing bankruptcy of the original mission of the California Master Plan for Higher Education to provide quality instruction for the people of the Golden State. Speaking as a graduate student, I and many of my fellow teaching assistants in history (who, unfortunately were *not* protected by our union from punitive action by departmental administrators if we chose to cancel classes), used the campus rebellions to illustrate how historical events have contemporary consequences but also how everyday students have the capacity to join together and alter the course of history. The goal behind educating the student body, be it through the text of protest chant or a classroom discussion of how the structural challenge to public education is linked to much larger historical issues, was to give students the tools to be intellectually and practically resilient. To borrow the words of an important Third World Movement mission, we "educate to liberate"—to help facilitate students' critique of the world around them, envision a better society, and do something to bring that vision into reality.

Collectivity, indeed, is a critical source of resiliency for all students. I learned this personally as my fellow TAs and I banded together to make use of these very pressing "teachable" moments. Likewise, progressive campus organizations, including IDEAS, provided necessary spaces for students to transform their personal experiences—as immigrants, as students, as members of the university community—into political action. In an era when immigrants and Ethnic Studies are coming under increasingly negative scrutiny, these collective spaces are critical in validating students' knowledge as a challenge to the status quo and a legitimate imagination for a better world.

Indeed, at the heart of my experiences with students in the midst of this economic turmoil has been a focus on the circulation and transformative power of alternative forms of knowledge against the backdrop of a crippling reality. Despite ephemeral prognostications that we are nearing the light at the end of the fiscal tunnel, student fees continue to rise. University of California President Mark Yudof, often criticized by students and outside observers for his exorbitant paycheck, has not minced words, stating that the UC can no longer direct equal energy towards maintaining a public university dedicated to affordability, accessibility, and excellence. At my campus, tutorial centers are closing, popular part-time instructors (particularly those who teach the languages of the Global South) are finding pink slips in their mailboxes, and when important purveyors of critical knowledge retire, such as the immensely important Ethnic Studies research librarian, their positions remain empty. Moreover, although the House of Representatives passed the DREAM Act in December of 2010; the Senate, even after tireless lobbying by students, quickly voted down the measure. Undocumented students continue to be persecuted and lined up for deportation. It appears that, in the time spanning my experiences thus far little has changed.

Despite the dour tenor of this environment, or perhaps because of it, knowledge production has become all the more necessary. As the architect of critical pedagogy Paulo Freire has outlined, revolution must be premised on the development of a critical consciousness. The immediate goals of the student activists I have encountered are simple: craft an affordable and relevant system of public education and enact some form of immigration reform to decriminalize undocumented students. These goals, however, are not an ultimate end. Indeed, the structures of power around us could easily co-opt and undermine these goals: "legalize" undocumented students and provide them and others with a sound education under the expectation they will in turn reproduce aggressive forms of capitalism while defending the neo-colonialist objectives of the nation-state. Rather, these goals, and the work that I attempt to do, as both a student and teacher, are means, strategies, and techniques for imagining a society liberated from the inequality with which we live today.

Education, as people of every shade of the political spectrum will attest, is a powerful tool. Through the discussion section, the teach-in, the speech at a march, the slogan emblazoned upon a t-shirt, the politicized note posted on Facebook, we seek to think through the logic that undergirds the power that oppresses our communities. These dialogues are never monolithic, nor do they propose easy answers. But, in connecting the history of militarism to the development of our contemporary immigrant communities or the rise of a post-modern economy to the skyrocketing costs of acquiring an education, we seek to situate our personal experiences within larger matrices of political, economic, and cultural formations of power. This critical understanding informs the next stages of organizing and action. The results might often be ambiguous, yet consciousness is something not easily taken away.

Although we may scour economic statistics in search of even the slightest glimmer of hope, public education will remain, in the meantime, an intensely personal site of contention where realities and dreams may collide. Students, however, are agents. As UCLA celebrates the fortieth anniversary of the establishment of Ethnic Studies on campus—a movement that relied on the energy and leadership of students of color—the struggle for a relevant and affordable education continues. And, as student activists then and now have illustrated, agency—cultivated through on-the-ground education and nurtured by peers—is not an abstract thought but a powerful reality. During many protests, to rouse the crowds, an organizer would ask "whose university?" Through the daily activism of students we are all emboldened to answer, "our university!"

Conclusion

Resilient Immigrants Resisting: Making It through the Many "Great Recessions"

Ana Sánchez-Muñoz

In this book we presented to the reader seventeen counter-stories of immigrants and their families facing difficult times due to The Great Recession. In doing so, we hoped to highlight the grounded knowledge among immigrant community members, whose stories and perspectives traditionally are, according to Daniel Solórzano and Tara Yosso, "epistemologically marginalized, silenced, and disempowered."[1] Overall, the stories provide important insight regarding the resilience strategies that immigrant families utilized, and can potentially employ, to navigate the financial crisis.

As we pointed out in the introduction, The Great Recession had, and continues to have, devastating effects on working-class and ethnic minority communities, particularly immigrants. The challenges and struggles depicted in these seventeen narratives reflect deeper social inequities within our society; hence the term used for the title of this conclusion "the many *Great Recessions*." The complex and varying ways in which immigrant communities are impacted by the current economic crisis thus requires a multi-level approach to the conceptualization and understanding of what we deem resilience. In this book, this approach

[1] Daniel Solórzano and Tara Yosso, "Critical Race Methodology: Counterstorytelling as an Analytical Framework for Education Research," *Qualitative Inquiry* 8 (2002): 36.

is manifested through the ways that family, institutional, and community-based networks are simultaneously relied upon by immigrants and their families to resist the social, economic, and political conditions that detrimentally affect them, and which are subsequently exacerbated by the financial crisis.

The first section focused on the family unit as a primary setting for developing resilience. In all these stories, families function as systems of support at many levels: financial, cultural, and emotional. While recognizing that familial practices influence minority students' academic and personal accomplishments, their stories also highlight the importance of financial aid and other types of federal and local assistance. Thus, the second section looked at the significant role that institutional support has in building immigrant resilience. Finally, the third section concentrated on community networks to support immigrants' resilience by providing economic, social, and cultural resources. Moreover, these networks became sites for resistance and transformation. Together, this multi-level approach attempts to show that resilience should not solely be considered as a characteristic that some individuals possess, but rather it should be understood as a strategy of resistance to larger structural conditions that marginalize immigrants in the United States and the capacity for people to transform ideological and structural hegemony.

A Multi-Level Approach

Arguably the most explicit challenge to the assumption of resilience as an individual process is the central role that family networks play within immigrant communities. Family support is a key factor in the ability of immigrants to materially and emotionally manage during difficult economic times. Family support fosters a collective resilience that enables members of the immigrant community to survive.

As Hyeyoung Kwon explains in her story of Korean workers in Los Angeles, many immigrants work long shifts, often taking two and even three jobs to make ends meet and ensure their children's future. Also, as many of the stories collected here reflect, education becomes not a right but an elusive dream when tuition fees go up and students need to take on multiple jobs to pay for college and everyday living expenses. Some, like Gabriela Habi in this book, have to leave school in order to work as much as possible to help their struggling families. Many others, such as Kevan Mocoso, are forced to reduce their course load and attend school only part time due to class cancellations and dramatic increases in enrollment fees. Adding to an already stressful situation, the possibility of losing one's job during the economic recession or not being able to find a new employment is a constant worry in many immigrants' lives. Yet, family support and resources often mediate such stresses.

While aspects of family support are present in other sections of the book, most prominent in the stories in section two was the role that institutional support had in shaping access to resources for immigrant families. Contributors in section two recognize the relationship between the availability of resources such as financial aid and public assistance, with the potential for immigrant families to thrive in dire times. Although there is a range in the types of institutional support highlighted in the stories, it is clear that the lack of such resources could have easily facilitated a different storytelling than that which was represented.

Since all the stories in the second section are told from the perspective of college students from immigrant families, varying forms of financial assistance provided by institutions of higher education are mentioned throughout and particularly highlighted by Roza Chirishyan, Abraham Rodriguez, and Julie Tran. Yet, Raymundo Hernández challenges the assumption of accessibility by discussing how undocumented immigrants are legally denied equal access to such resources. Further, Esther Hansook Oh and Robert Beam's compelling narratives of institutional support, like mental health services and public assistance programs, represent the complexity of immigrant family experiences and leave readers to view the necessity of resources that mediate structural inequalities embedded in American society.

It is not only important to recognize how these working class, minority students and their families stay afloat despite the financial meltdown, but we must emphasize how many are actively involved in striving for social justice and helping others as well. The third section focuses on what some researchers have called *resilient resistance*[2] or *transformational resistance*[3]—that which has the greatest possibility for social change. The stories of resilience shared by the immigrant contributors in this book are examples of resistance in that they encompass a critique of social inequality and a desire to create social change.

It is nothing short of amazing that immigrant families are able to overcome so many adversities against all odds and be successful (e.g., attending graduate school, like Jean-Paul deGuzmán, or surviving foreclosures and layoffs, like Anita

[2] Tara Yosso, "A Critical Race and LatCrit Approach to Media Literacy: Chicana/o Resistance to Visual Microaggressions." Unpublished doctoral dissertation, University of California, Los Angeles.

[3] Daniel Solórzano and Dolores Delgado Bernal, "Examining Transformational Resistance through a Critical race and LatCrit Theory Framework. Chicana and Chicano Student in an Urban Context," *Urban Education* 36, no. 2 (2001): 308–342.

Arce). Resilient working-class students, like Raymundo Hernández and others, are protesting against the dismantling of public education, demonstrating against fee hikes, organizing for labor rights, and fundraising to help support the fight against racist laws (such as Arizona Senate Bill 1070 and House Bill 2281), among other activities of resistance on and off campus. They are **resilient** because they have overcome many obstacles in their journey to make it in the "land of opportunities" so far. They are **resistant** because they do not succumb to the racist stereotypes or add to the number of youth who has been pushed out of school and into the prison pipeline. Instead, they are motivated to do their part to defy the statistics and pave the way for a brighter future for immigrants and students of color, in general. The ability to survive and, moreover, succeed is a strategic response to the oppression that immigrant communities face.

Our approach is demonstrative of the four functions of counter-stories.[4] The first is to humanize the experiences of marginalized people and the subsequent potential to build community among immigrants and their allies. While The Great Recession is an economic phenomenon, the stories remind us how disparate conditions affect people and set the context for solidarity building. Second, counter-stories highlight the social, political, and economic contexts shaping disparities among communities of color in an attempt to challenge normative, and oftentimes deficit, explanations of these conditions. In our focus on resilience, the stories challenge readers to consider the assets of immigrant communities and the structural issues they attempt to resist. Third, counter-stories serve to emphasize how members of marginalized communities are not alone in their experiences and desire for change; and fourth, they teach community members and allies that there are possibilities for alternative realities.

While people throughout the United States anticipate a time in which the economy will gain some semblance to the prosperity that so many associate with this country, many immigrants are aware that their ability to prosper is limited by institutional barriers that prevent their equal participation. Yet, as immigrant families continue to struggle against the devastating impact of social, political, and economic inequalities, they develop and demonstrate an unwavering resilience and spirit that provide hope for a more just society. Thus, what we hope readers gain most from this collection of counter-stories is a greater sense of the transformative possibilities offered throughout the narratives and for the future.

---

[4] Ibid., 32

Bibliography

Solórzano, Daniel, and Dolores Delgado Bernal. "Examining Transformational Resistance through a Critical race and LatCrit Theory Framework. Chicana and Chicano Student in an Urban Context." *Urban Education* 36, no. 2 (2001): 308–342. DOI: 10.1177/0042085901363002.

Solórzano, Daniel, and Tara J. Yosso. "Critical Race Methodology: Counterstorytelling as an Analytical Framework for Education Research." *Qualitative Inquiry,* 8 (2002): 23–44. DOI: 10.1177/107780040200800103.

Yosso, Tara J. "A Critical Race and LatCrit Approach to Media Literacy: Chicana/o Resistance to Visual Microaggressions." Unpublished doctoral dissertation, University of California, Los Angeles, 2000.

ABOUT OUR CO-EDITORS

Ana Sánchez-Muñoz

I was born in Spain. I graduated from the University of Salamanca with a B.A. in philology (major in English linguistics and literatures of the English-speaking countries with minors in French and Italian). I came to the United States in 2000, and I have been living in Los Angeles since then. I started my doctoral studies in 2001, and I graduated from the University of Southern California in 2007 with a Ph.D. in Hispanic linguistics. My research interests include language variation and change, bilingualism, language acquisition, and situations of language contact. In particular, I am interested in situations of contact between Spanish and English in the United States and in studying how Spanish is developed, used, and maintained by heritage speakers of Spanish in the United States. Currently, I am an assistant professor in the Department of Chicana/o Studies at California State University, Northridge (CSUN), where I teach language acquisition and language development in Chicana/o and ESL speakers. I am also a faculty member of the linguistics program at CSUN.

Tracy Lachica Buenavista

I am a second-generation Pinay and was born and raised in the San Francisco Bay Area. My upbringing conditioned in me an immense desire to contribute to the social, economic, and political well-being of my family and community. Thus, I pursued higher education and earned a B.A. in biology and minor in Ethnic Studies from U.C. Berkeley. Ethnic Studies changed my life because everything I learned was dangerously relevant, and I hoped to share with others the transformative possibilities that educational attainment can provide. After receiving an M.A. in Asian American Studies at San Francisco State University and a Ph.D. in Education at UCLA, I am now an assistant professor in the Department of Asian American Studies at California State University, Northridge, where I teach courses and conduct research on race and racism and the educational experiences of U.S. Pilipina/os and other underserved communities of color.

Eunai Shrake

I was born in Korea and came to the United States as an international student for my graduate degree. I graduated from UCLA in 1996, with a Ph.D. in education with a concentration on social sciences and comparative education. I am currently an associate professor in the Department of Asian American Studies at California State University, Northridge, where I teach courses on multicultural education with a special emphasis on Asian American students and their culture. My research focuses on cross-cultural studies in the areas of parenting styles, ethnic identity development, and adolescent problem behaviors.

Gina Masequesmay

I was born in Saigon, Vietnam, and left the country for France when I was six years old. My family moved to France and then to the United States in late 1977. I grew up in the "Valley" and only moved out when I went to Pomona College in Claremont. I graduated in 1991, with a B.A. in sociology and decided to try out social work for two years. I returned to school, enrolling in a graduate program in sociology at UCLA. I earned my Ph.D. in 2001 and began teaching at California State University, Northridge (CSUN) three days after I filed my dissertation. My research interests are on immigrant adaptation, Vietnamese Americans, and the intersection of race, ethnicity, class, gender, and sexuality. I am now associate professor in Asian American Studies, where I served as interim chair in 2007.

www.ingramcontent.com/pod-product-compliance
Lightning Source LLC
LaVergne TN
LVHW082351200926
848481LV00012B/3530
* 9 7 8 0 7 5 7 5 9 5 3 8 7 *